Racing Bicycles

Racing Bicycles

The Illustrated Story of Road Cycling

Nick Higgins

Laurence King Publishing

Published in 2018
by Laurence King Publishing Ltd
361–373 City Road
London EC1V 1LR
Tel: +4420 7841 6900
Fax: +44 20 7841 6910
Email: enquiries@laurenceking.com
www.laurenceking.com

A catalogue record for this book
is available from the British Library.
ISBN: 978-1-78627-166-2

Design: Alexandre Coco
Copy-editing: Jessica Spencer

Printed in China

10 9 8 7 6 5 4 3 2 1

FRONTISPIECE
King of the Mountains
Richard Virenque, France's great
hope of the 1990s, in the *maillot
à pois*, 1999.

Introduction

On the western side of the Col de Menté in the French Pyrenees there is a memorial stone set in the rock above the road at the apex of a hairpin bend:

Lundi 12 juillet 1971
Tragédie dans le
TOUR DE FRANCE
Sur cette route transforme en
torrent de boue par un orage
d'apocalypse, Luis Ocaña,
maillot jaune, abandonnait
tous ses espoirscontres ce rocher

Monday 12 July 1971
Tragedy in the Tour de France
On this road transformed into a
torrent of mud by an apocalyptic
storm Luis Ocaña, yellow jersey,
abandoned all his hopes
against this rock.

It marks the most famous crash in Tour de France history. The weather was apocalyptic, and the crushing of Ocaña's ambition was operatic, his cruel punishment for presuming to challenge Merckx's reign.

In 2014 I was in the south of France, looking for a ride for the day. I saw a promisingly wriggling line on the map and rode across the Garonne Valley to Aspet, and then on to the foot of the climb. Only when I started up the incline did I realize where I had brought myself: the Col de Menté, the scene of Ocaña's epic failure. It would be easy to miss the memorial stone if you were not looking for it, which would be a shame – the poetic indulgence of the inscription matches perfectly the cultural qualities of the sport it memorializes.

You can't inadvertently find yourself knocking a ball into the net at Wembley, and you can't absentmindedly drive yourself around the Nürburgring. But you can ride the same mountain that Ocaña rode, and take the same corner. I was luckier with the weather. It was a charmed moment, to arrive at the bend that I been watching in grainy black-and-white footage for months before. I knew what the men who held Luis after his crash looked like, and I had watched the man in shorts with an umbrella run through the spray to watch him after the fall, over and over again. Not only is this a warning against overplanning, but it is a story of the charm of the bicycle – and the race, and the places where the races have been, and the history left behind. If you love bicycles, and you love riding them, and you love watching them raced, you can in certain places put yourself breathtakingly close to the best moments of the sport. You can be made to realize just how slow, old and gravity bound you are when you struggle to reach the observatory on the top of Mont Ventoux. For all the hours of watching races on television, it was only after riding up the Tourmalet that I properly understood what I had been seeing.

As well as a story of riders and races, there is the history of a machine. The bicycle was an answer to the most fundamental of needs: to move from one place to another. Having devised a technology to meet a very practical need, inevitably human nature demanded that it would be raced, and that unleashed another competition as inventors, artisans and engineers developed the machine into its most efficient and effective form. The charm of the bicycle is that it is a relatively simple machine, and the refinement of its parts to deliver maximum performance from a minimally complicated device is a fascinating process. The elegance of an efficient mechanism and the sculptural beauty of well-designed parts meet in the bicycle. Something as plainly functional as a lug attains an iconic charm, an almost mystically seductive attraction. The evolution of the bicycle has its dead ends and its great leaps forward, every one witnessed in the frames, parts and products that make up the history of the bike.

And then there are the clothes. From the wool and tweed of pioneer cyclists to the absurd graphic chaos of the modern helmet-to-overshoe branded peloton it is the most sartorially sophisticated sport in the world. A traditional

Italian leather cycling shoe has all the elegance and poignancy of a ballet slipper, while the bile-coloured fluorescent lycra of Tinkoff had all the brash confidence of the best pop art.

In this book I try to make a record of all these things: the excitement of watching races as they unroll, and the endless archive of drama, tragedy and barely credible anecdote that makes up the history of the sport. The fascination with the contest is amplified by the compelling phenomenon of the bicycle as an object, and the vivid spectacle that has been made of the competitions contrived for it.

There is archive footage of Buster Keaton riding a Draisienne, there is real-time onboard camera recording from inside the peloton as it races today, and there is everything in between. I have tried to get down in my words and pictures the things that have seized my imagination in all this rich mix: the resonant artefacts of the kit, the compelling narratives of the races and the stories of the riders themselves. Cycling is notoriously divided into its factions, but I hope there will be something here to satisfy any niche curiosity.

As well as all this armchair study of the records and the relics, I hope I have retained the link with the incomparable physical adventure of actually riding a bicycle.

The epitome of the sporting bicycle: built by Ernesto Colnago and ridden by Eddy Merckx to take the World Hour Record in Mexico City, 1972. Steel frame with drillium parts.

Vélo

Constantly developing but always familiar,
the bicycle is a story of evolution, technical
successes adopted, innovative failures left
obsolete. Most of the familiar parts of the bicycle
had been conceived before 1900, though many
were not developed to the point where they would
be usable until long after that. New materials
and techniques have made possible ever lighter,
stronger and faster bicycles, with equipment
that controls them with a power and subtlety
unimaginable to the early makers. The essential
device, however, remains the same – and it is an
unavoidable truth that the most important part
on a bike is your legs.

A Bit of History

I n the past two hundred or so years, the bicycle has evolved from a horse-headed hobby cart to a sub-7kg (15lb) race bike. The driving force behind its invention was the need for a convenient replacement for the horse. Up until the late 1800s, the only improvement on human mobility was to ride, or have an animal pull your cart for you. As a tribute to the technology it would replace, many early frames had a carved horse's head badge at the front, but this quickly died out.

The Célérifère, an unarticulated wooden beam framing two cartwheels, carved with the head of a mythical beast, was the first attempt to depose the horse. It was devised by Comte de Sivrac in 1790. An earlier device, allegedly drawn up by Leonardo da Vinci, is probably a mischievous early twentieth-century forgery, possibly by Italian Futurists trying to wrest the heritage of the bicycle from the French.

The next step was Baron Karl Drais von Sauerbronn's Laufmaschine (running machine). Better known as the Draisienne, it comprised two wagon wheels under a steerable wooden frame, with a rudimentary friction brake. Numerous versions followed, notably from Nicéphore Niépce, the Frenchman who also invented

Célérifère,
early nineteenth century

photography, the internal-combustion engine, and a pump to supply water to the palace of Versailles. The devices acquired the name Dandyhorse and their riders a reputation for recklessness.

All over Europe the attraction of horseless transport inspired innovation and investment. After some experiments with treadles, the pedal was devised to directly power the wheel, making the action of the foot against the ground obsolete. This development is credited to Pierre Michaux in 1860.

The Ordinary

A pair of pedals turning an axle rigidly fixed to the front wheel meant one revolution advanced the machine by

Draisienne,
early nineteenth century

OPPOSITE
Ordinary, 1873

The Safety

The limits of a direct-drive wheel were overcome by the introduction of a chain driven by a toothed ring sprocket turning another sprocket mounted on the wheel. These were first made by Harry Lawson in 1879, but patented and made commercially successful by James Starley, a prolific inventor and businessman from Coventry. Starley's Ariel was perhaps the first modern, commercially manufactured bicycle. This was followed by the Rover, designed by his son, John Kemp Starley. These models were called Safety bicycles to distinguish them from the less safe Ordinaries.

As frame builders searched for the most efficient, and least precarious, configuration, various designs were offered, including the Extraordinary, the Whippet, the Facile and the Kangaroo. The willingness to experiment with radical forms has been a constant feature of bicycle design, and many 'hopeful monsters' are scattered across the evolution of the bicycle.

ABOVE
James Starley's Safety bicycle, first patented in 1884

BELOW LEFT
Extraordinary, 1888

BELOW RIGHT
Racing Ordinaries, late 1800s

OPPOSITE:
1. Lawson, 1877
2. Kangaroo, 1884
3. Bantam 'Crypto', 1894
4. Peugeot 'Lion', 1892
5. Moser, 1988
6. Whippet, 1885
7. Gitane, 1987
8. Pinarello, 1997

just one circumference of the wheel: not a great rate of travel, unless that circumference was abnormally large. So the front wheel grew outrageously while the rear shrank, eventually resulting in the Ordinary, or Penny Farthing. All that limited the drive now was the inside leg of the rider. It was at this point that the term 'bicycle' was coined, probably in France.

The Penny Farthing was a huge, but notorious, popular success. Its extreme configuration and effective acceleration delivered a precarious machine attractive to reckless riders. Casually organized races attracted daring enthusiasts keen to demonstrate their mastery of the innovative device.

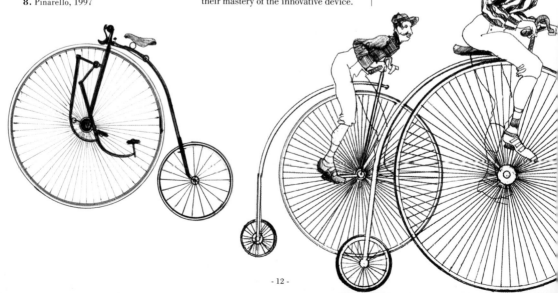

Frames

BELOW
In the early 1860s French
mechanics devised the pedal,
turning the Draisienne into
the Velocipede.

OPPOSITE
A selection of lugs.

Wood

As the bicycle was born out of horse-
drawn technology – cart building –
it was wood that was used to make
the first machines. While it is light,
workable, and easy to produce, its
strengths are limited, and the properties of metal quickly made timber
obsolete for frames, though wheels
were still wooden until the 1930s.

Iron

Iron was the only option for the first
metal bikes. It was better than wood
in some ways, but, until some way
of making a hollow tube could be
devised, impossibly heavy.

Steel

A cast-iron bike could weigh up to
36kg (80lb), so, as soon as was technically possible, hollow steel tubing
was used. In 1855 German brothers
Max and Reinhard Mannesmann,
while trying to find a way to harden
the cotter pins holding their cranks

on, stumbled across the technique of tube rolling, passing a solid bar between two rollers to form a tube with a central void. Hollow, seamless steel tubes offered the combination of strength and lighter weight that bicycle makers had been waiting for. The tubing could be made with the optimum ratio of diameter-to-wall thickness, and lengths could be thickened towards the joints. The perfect material for bikes had arrived. Iron combined with other metals makes a material of subtle and various qualities, and alloys of steel were developed to make frames as light and as strong as possible. As processes gained in sophistication, the bicycle became a finer, lighter machine, and for the first hundred years it was from steel alone that makers formed the best racing bicycles.

Steel is invested with almost mystical properties. It is accepted that it can have a soul, and a life, and an animated 'responsiveness' unlike any other material.

The use of alloys has led to an inscrutable coding of frame materials, which actually indicates the relative proportions of their constituent metals. For years the mantra of the serious cyclist was '531', the ratio of manganese, carbon and molybdenum, the three elements alloyed with iron. Other ratios are also available – 501, 753, 500, 525, 631 and 953 – each offering subtly different qualities of performance.

Frame builders

The early racing-bicycle industry was based around artisan frame builders. Craft engineers built individual steel frames and components, which were finished in small factories.

The craft of the frame builder is legendary. Even as they went into mass production, the reputation of names such as Masi, Colnago and Pegoretti was born out of their skill as individual frame builders.

The name on the frame, though, was often not the actual maker of the bike. Contractual obligations might have dictated the livery, but riders chose the best bike for their purpose. Lance Armstrong's Trek was sometimes actually a Lynskey; Laurent Fignon's Raleigh was made by Cyfac. Eddy Merckx's World Hour Record bike of 1972 is famously by Ernesto Colnago, but the badge says Windsor, an opportunistic and largely forgotten Mexican manufacturer.

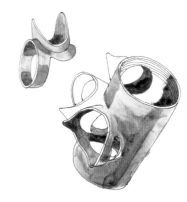

Lugs

Tubes were first put together using lugs, steel forms into which each tube of the frame is inserted and then welded in place. The lugs became the place where the most extrovert frame builders demonstrated their skills: flamboyant arabesques and gothic chevrons embellish their junctions, picked out with meticulous coach lining. As welding and tube-rolling technologies improved, it became cheaper – and lighter – to weld tubes directly to each other, with the walls thickened or butted at the ends to give strength to the join. While lugs have become rare on steel bikes, they have made a comeback as a way of assembling carbon frames, where separate carbon elements are joined rather than the frame being moulded in one piece.

Paris Diamant, the first winner of the Tour de France, 1903.

Aluminium

Aluminium was used to build bikes as early as 1890. The LuMiNum was a one-piece cast frame, made in America. Production stopped when World War II took up all available metal and it was not until the late 1930s that, mainly French, manufacturers offered bikes made from what they called Duralumin (also duraluminum, duraluminium, duralum, duralium or dural). It is not an easy metal to weld, which led to some interesting lugged, screwed, bolted, wedged and glued constructions. The French Caminade bikes of that period were made from octagonal tubing screwed into beautifully cast aluminium lugs. Alloys of aluminium with copper, magnesium and silicon are not as strong as steel, but are a third lighter. This weight advantage meant that it flourished in the peloton of the 1990s, until it was pushed aside by the irresistible qualities of carbon. Aluminium is commonly believed to deliver a harsh ride, and it has never inspired the affection that frame builders have for steel. It is generally accepted that aluminium has no soul.

Titanium

Half the weight of steel and just as strong, titanium is mainly used in the aerospace industries. It was a rare and unusual metal until the 1970s, when a downturn in aviation released more of the metal onto the market. The British firm Speedwell commissioned Lamborghini to weld titanium frames for them in the 1960s. It is a difficult material to work with, demanding very particular conditions to be successfully welded, and the frames were hugely expensive when they were first built. Not until the 1980s did price and demand allow a significant number of frames to be made from titanium. Tubing was only available in a limited range of diameters, so some titanium frames were built from sheet metal shaped by hand over forms. This explains the unusual configuration of Bianchi's TT bikes around 1996.

Titanium was not easy to see on the professional circuit, and seemingly shy when it did appear, but Luis Ocaña rode a titanium Speedwell, badged as a Motobécane, when he won the Tour de France in 1973, and in the 1990s Lance Armstrong rode Lynskey titanium bikes, some badged as Trek, others as Eddy Merckx.

Pinarello Dogma, as used by
Chris Froome, 2013

Carbon

Carbon is the all-conquering material of modern cycling, attractive for its high strength to weight ratio, its rigidity, and its capacity to be formed into any shape you can design. It is a composite material: a matrix and a reinforcement. Though the word is never used, what people prefer to call 'carbon' is technically a plastic. Long strands of carbon filament – poly-acrylonitrile – are woven into sheets and laid in a mould, where a binding resin is applied. The raw material is infinitely malleable, but sets into a rigid lightweight frame – or shoe, chainring, seat post, wheel or spoke, just about anything that does not need to bend. Early frames were made by fixing carbon tubes into alloy lugs, but their bonds were unreliable, and a bike that came to pieces mid-race was never a viable contender. A robust lugless, mould-made bike was developed by 1986, and from then on the advance of carbon was unstoppable. Now frames can be made in a mould or built from separate carbon components: tubes lugged with either cabon or metal, or mitred and joined with sheet carbon, wrapped and set in an oven.

The moulded formation of a carbon frame has freed it from the restrictions of being configured from tubes, allowing one-piece monocoque forms. These flourished during the 1990s and 2000, but were legislated out of record attempts and competition by the Union Cycliste Internationale (UCI) to try to maintain a sport where human capability is tested rather than technology. This means a race-legal

LOOK KG 396
Carbon aero frame, 2000

bicycle frame must be made up of two diamond shapes sharing a common edge. Carbon's mould-made multiples make the economics of production as attractive to manufacturers as the nature of the material is to its riders. Metal will always require skilled working, and while the artisan frame builder might be the revered craftsman of the bicycle world, in competition carbon is king.

The last steel bike to win the Tour de France was Miguel Induráin's Pinarello in 1994. After that, aluminium flourished briefly before being overtaken by carbon. Now that it is possible to make a bike below the minimum 6.8kg (15lb) legal racing weight, the only improvements to the frame are in aerodynamics, and carbon's nature allows infinite variations of form in pursuit of the most discreet profile.

Wheels

The wheels of early bicycles were taken straight from a cart, with wooden spokes supporting iron-clad wooden rims, turning on a bearingless hub. The spokes supported the hub from underneath only, and if they were made thinner to save weight, they were likely to break. A wheel built on tensioned wire spokes was devised for aviation by George Cayley in 1808, but it was not until 1870 that they were adopted for bicycles. The wheel became a pre-stressed dynamic structure, far lighter and much stronger than the primitive wagon wheel. Wire spokes also made possible wheels of extreme diameter, allowing the Ordinary to achieve its radical configuration.

Forces of compression and tension work through the wheel in ways that still perplex engineers, but they produce a brilliantly efficient support and transmission for acceleration or braking. Physics also dictates that any part of the bicycle that has to be rotated as it moves will demand more energy than a part that just travels in a straight line. This means, unsurprisingly, that light wheels are best. Developments in wheels have to balance saving weight with retaining strength.

Wooden rims continued as standard until the 1930s. Beech, birch or maple laminates were used to build rims, mould-formed and then machined to the correct profile. Wood, however, as an organic material, is unstable, vulnerable even to changes in the weather, and had to be carefully maintained. In 1931 Antonin Magne raced on alloy rims, painted to look like wood to conceal the innovation. In 1934 he won the Tour de France on Duralumin rims, an alloy of copper and aluminium, and the use of alloy persisted until carbon arrived in the 1990s.

The form of the wheel affects its performance: a smooth surface creates less turbulence as it moves through the air. Disc wheels were made as early as 1896, but only in the 1980s were they seriously developed for racing, usually for the velodrome or in time trialling. The disc can be a cover over a conventionally built wheel, or composed from sheet material, resin or carbon. In the open, though, cross-winds make a disc unstable. A disc with large holes in it has been offered as a compromise. Deep rims, with fewer spokes, either steel or carbon, have become the usual form.

Lacing

A cartwheel had radial lacing – spokes running directly from the hub to the rim, each a radius of the wheel. James Starley was the first to arrange his spokes away from the flat plane of the wheel, using two sets, one seated on each side of the hub. This made a wheel with lateral strength. He went on to devise tangential lacing in 1874, where each spoke runs from the hub at a tangent, crossing others on its way to the rim. This configuration is more effective in transferring power – both acceleration and braking – from the hub to the rim. Since the drive is only to the back wheel, it is common to have a radially laced front and tangentially laced rear, giving a slight weight advantage and possibly a little less drag.

Lacing patterns continue to be various, contrived either for efficiency or aesthetics. The mystery of the wheel's physics allows endless debate as to the ideal configuration. The spokes themselves are steel, sometimes bladed for better aerodynamics. Inevitably, though, it is carbon fibre that constantly challenges steel to improve performance.

Radial

Tangential

OPPOSITE
Spoked, disc, bladed, perforated, radial, carbon steel and Duralumin: a variety of wheels exhibiting different qualities.

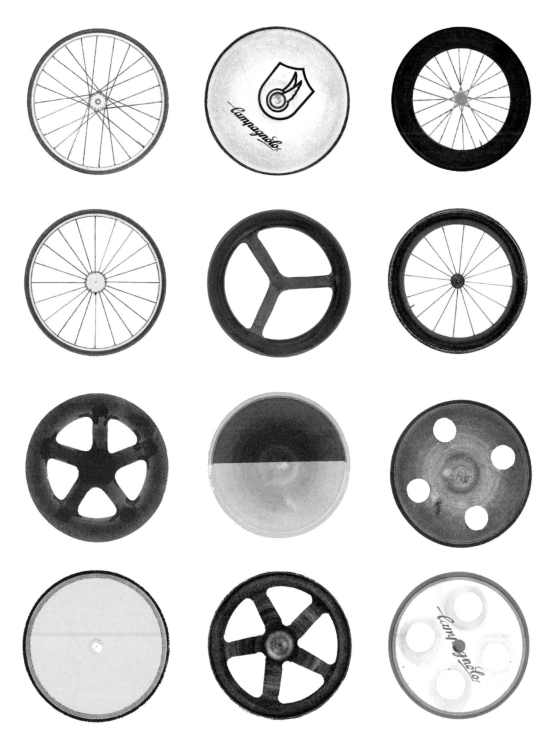

Tyres

First there were iron bands on the Draisienne, next solid rubber rims on the Ordinary, and then, at last, in 1887 John Dunlop brought relief with the pneumatic tyre. Very soon afterwards, Édouard Michelin made them removable. Between them they contrived the most persistent feature of cycling: the puncture. Early racers, banned from accepting outside assistance, wore tubular tyres wrapped around their shoulders like bandoliers. Even in 2012 it was still possible to sabotage the Tour de France with a bag of nails. Dunlop's pneumatic tyre has ensured an ongoing history of riders standing by the road with a wheel held in the air, and domestiques giving up wheels for their star riders.

Tubular tyres cemented onto the rims are still the racing standard, being lighter than the clincher and capable of inflation to higher pressures. On a clincher the edge of the tyre, strengthened by steel wire 'beads', is held under a flange on the rim. They are simpler to use, but lack the mystique of a tyre that has to be sewn around its inner tube and then glued to the rim.

In 1930 Tullio Campagnolo invented the quick-release axle to get the wheel off faster when it punctured and to turn it around when a choice between two sprockets was the closest thing they had to gears.

Air

So why not a solid tyre? Never stand on the verge again holding a wheel in the air while you watch the peloton race away.

Three reasons: first, air under high pressure absorbs road vibrations ideally without any weight penalty. Second, the rolling resistance of any solid tyre is higher than a pneumatic because a greater mass of solid material is deformed, while at the same time the reduced area of contact between road and tyre gives less grip. And finally, weight, just where you don't want it, and rotational weight, the worst sort. So air remains the ride of choice.

A pneumatic tyre: the persistently vulnerable contact point with the road.

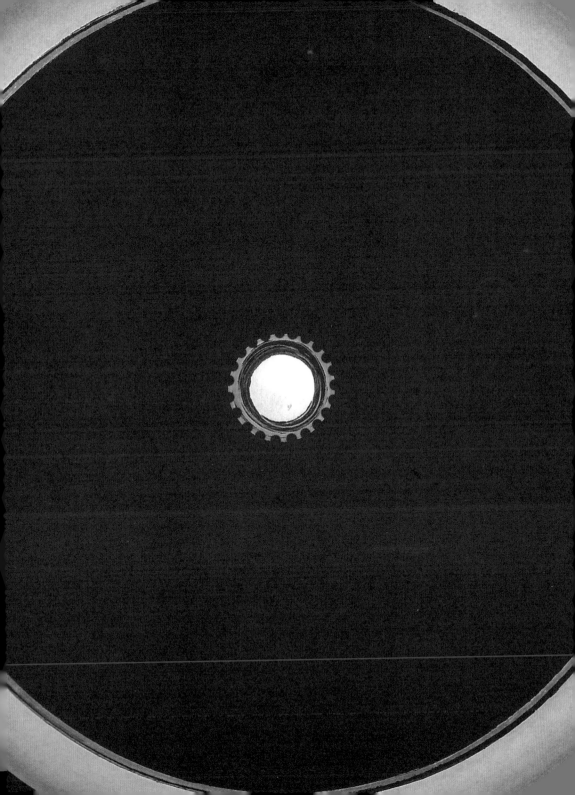

Chains

In the 1880s, a chain drive was devised to transmit power from the pedal to the wheel. The Meyer-Guilmet bike of 1869 was possibly the first, though Henry Lawson's machine ten years later is seen as the first successful chain-drive bicycle.

Using a chain to bring the force from the rider's leg to the wheel allowed the ratio of pedal rotation to wheel-turning to be determined by the relative size of the two toothed sprockets. The Ordinary was obsolete.

The first chains were 'block chains', where links were built from solid steel blocks connected by pins through chain plates on each side. The spacing between the sprocket teeth was wider to allow for the length of the block. In 1883 Hans Renold, a Swiss living in Manchester, invented the Renold Roller Chain, in which the links overlapped and the rivet passed through a roller, making a low-friction, lightweight chain. This pattern has remained the standard ever since. On track bikes the block chain did persist for some time, though, riders claiming that the immense loads produced by their acceleration necessitated a stronger chain. These were called 'inch pitch' chains.

The chain pitch – the distance from one pin centre to the next – was universally standardized at ½in as the block chain disappeared in the mid-1950s. Only Shimano attempted an alternative, making a doomed effort to introduce a 10mm chain in the 1970s. Width between the plates has varied, from ⁵⁄₁₆in to ⅟₃₃in, narrowing to accommodate more sprockets on the cassette. Imperial measurements persist in bicycle transmissions.

Some of the first chain drives were mounted on the left-hand side of the bike, but right-hand drive quickly became universal so that any turning forces tended to tighten rather than loosen the right-hand threaded bolts that held everything together. It was the Wright Brothers who in 1900 devised a left-hand threaded bolt to ensure the same conditions applied for the non-drive-side pedal.

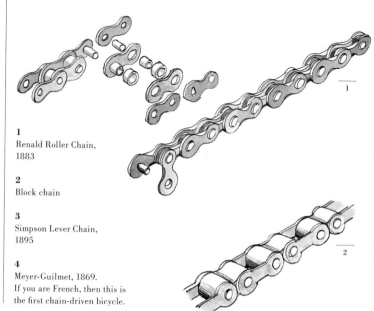

1
Renald Roller Chain, 1883

2
Block chain

3
Simpson Lever Chain, 1895

4
Meyer-Guilmet, 1869.
If you are French, then this is the first chain-driven bicycle.

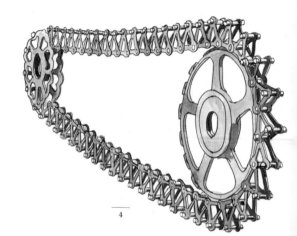

Freewheels

A bicycle that cannot freewheel is hard to control. The implications of this are particularly important when going down hills: Ordinaries were fitted with footrests to allow the rider to avoid the spinning pedals. The freewheel allows the pedals to be kept still while the bicycle is in motion so that the bike can coast. In 1821 Briton Lewis Gompertz, vegan, pioneer of animal rights, and inventor, devised the first known ratchet to allow the front wheel of his Draisienne to be powered by his arms.

In 1869 in the United States, William Van Anden invented a freewheel with a single spring-loaded ratchet driving the front wheel. The device was adopted reluctantly in Britain, where riders preferred to persist with their fixed-wheel Ordinaries, but eventually all bikes would have them (except on the track, where conditions suit a fixed wheel). The drive moved to the back wheel, and the mechanism of the freewheel developed into a set of spring-loaded pawls. These pawls engage with teeth in the hub when turned in one direction, but move back on their springs when the pedals are held still or turned backwards. The pedals can turn the hub, but the hub cannot turn the pedals. To begin with the mechanism was built into the gears of the bike and was known as a freewheel; later, it was relocated to the hub, where it became known as a freehub.

TOP
Sprocket

MIDDLE
Block

BOTTOM
Cassette

Gears and Derailleurs

The first races were ridden on single-speed bikes, walked uphill when riders could no longer turn the pedals. A second sprocket added to the other side of the wheel allowed a second gear, but riders had to get off and turn the wheel around in the frame to use it. Later, a pair of sprockets adjacent to each other gave more ratios, the chain being lifted from one to the other by hand. It was better, but you still had get off to change up or down.

Since well before 1900 makers had been trying to devise an effective way of offering a range of gears. Hundreds of patents were filed, most of them hopeless. In France Jean Loubeyre's Polycélère of 1895 is considered to be the first derailleur gear. In Britain, however, it is held to be E.H. Hodgkinson's Gradient, despite its 1896 patent.

The first effective derailleur was made in 1905, by Paul de Vivie. Known as Vélocio, he was an inspirational pioneer of bicycle riding, a vegetarian and Esperanto speaker who was provoked into improving his ability to climb after being passed on the Col de la République by a man smoking a pipe. He experimented with various mechanisms, including a chain on either side of the bike. His derailleur eventually offered four speeds, deflecting the chain between two sprockets at either end of its action.

Once the principle had been introduced, the method for directing the chain across its sprockets was refined by various makers. While even the earliest mechanisms bore a close resemblance to the familiar derailleur, there were other ideas. The exquisite aluminium Caminargent of the 1930s had a Caminade mechanism whereby the chain remained in line while the three-speed cog moved across beneath it.

Most notable of these unconventional designs was Campagnolo's remarkable Cambio Corsa system, introduced in 1946. A lever released the toothed rear axle allowing it to move along a matching toothed dropout, using the travel of the whole back wheel to re-tension the chain, rather than the spring-loaded jockey wheel preferred by seemingly every other system. A 'striker' above the chain moved it sideways to locate the desired cog. At first operated with two rods on the seat stay, one releasing the back wheel while the other realigned the chain, it was later refined to a single rod moving first the axle and then the chain as it was turned. Deploying the Cambio Corsa required a careful sequence of adjustments and backpedalling. As unlikely as it seems, it was ridden successfully in major races, notably by Gino Bartali.

In 1932 Swiss track and road champion Oscar Egg developed the Osgear, the most viable mechanism for moving the chain across multiple cogs. A cage mounted on the chainstay and operated by a lever on the down tube pushed the chain across the sprockets. A spring-loaded pulley wheel mounted below the chainstay took up the tension in the chain. And this was all accomplished without having to get off.

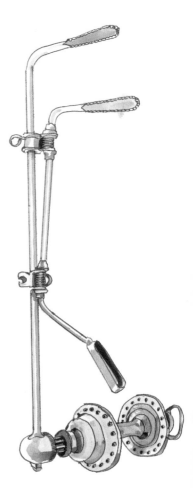

Campagnolo Cambio Corsa, 1946

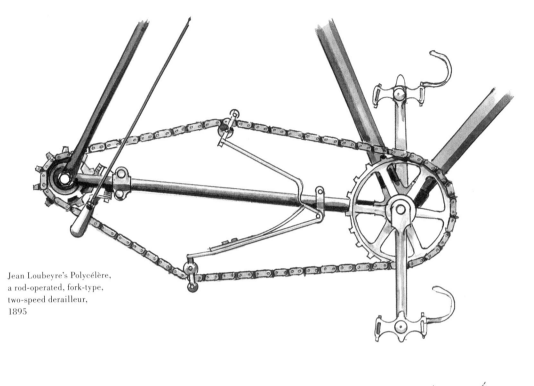

Jean Loubeyre's Polycélère,
a rod-operated, fork-type,
two-speed derailleur,
1895

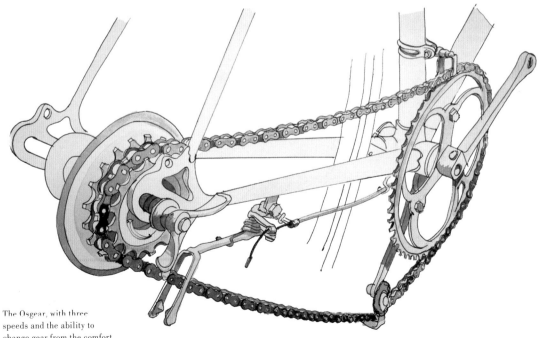

The Osgear, with three
speeds and the ability to
change gear from the comfort
of your seat!
1932

Nivex parallelogram derailleur, six speeds, 1938

In spite of the inevitable arguments over earlier patents and the rival claims of forgotten competitors, the first derailleur that worked by moving the chain with an articulated parallelogram (called a cage) operated by cables was made by Nivex in 1938. Mounted on the chainstay, its parallelogram pivoted on a vertical rather than a horizontal axis, and offered precise, accurate shifting.

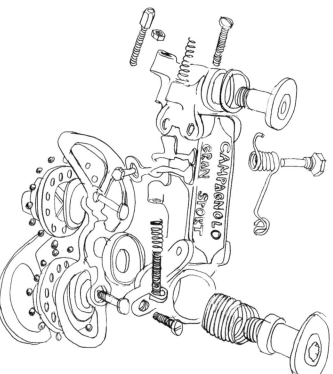

Campagnolo Gran Sport parallelogram derailleur, 1951

Campagnolo's Gran Sport became the first mass-produced parallelogram derailleur, and remained the component of choice until the 1960s. The first model used two cables, a single-cable parallelogram derailleur arriving in 1951.

From the 1940s Campagnolo dominated the manufacture of racing equipment. Only in the 1980s did Shimano start to offer a competitive alternative. The history of component production is one of attrition for the small artisan engineer–makers who were overwhelmed by the manufacturing giants. Nivex, Suntour, Osgear, Cyclo, Suwe, L'As: all disappeared as the small workshop gave way to the multinationals.

Nivex, the original parallelogram,
1938

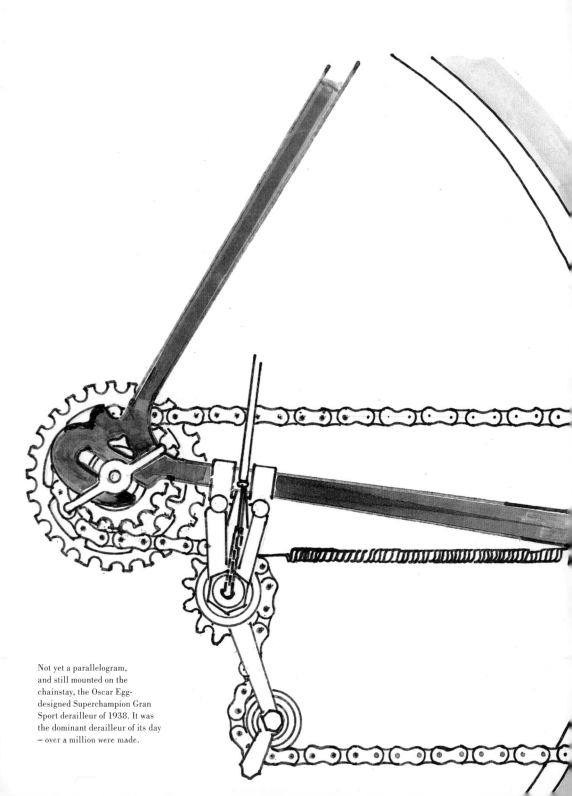

Not yet a parallelogram,
and still mounted on the
chainstay, the Oscar Egg-
designed Superchampion Gran
Sport derailleur of 1938. It was
the dominant derailleur of its day
— over a million were made.

Measuring gears

As soon as gears offered a choice of ratios, it became useful to have a system to determine how far your pedalling would take you, and how hard it was going to be to get there. It is where mathematics meets cycling, and several measures have been used.

The imperial measure, gear inches, was originally just the diameter of an Ordinary's drive wheel in inches. Complicated by the Safety bicycle's gears, it became the number of teeth on the chainring divided by the number on the sprocket, then multiplied by the diameter of the drive wheel in inches. This produces one number, an index of mechanical advantage.

Metres of development, the metric measure, is calculated exactly the same way, just using metres instead of inches, but then multiplying your number by π. Again, it arrives at a single figure, but perhaps a more meaningful one in that it identifies an actual distance.

Some claim that gain ratio is a more thorough measure of a bicycle's performance in that it includes crank length in the calculation: the radius of the drive wheel is divided by the length of the pedal crank multiplied by the number of teeth in the front chainring divided by the number of teeth in the rear sprocket. This gives the ratio between the distance travelled by the bicycle and the distance travelled by a pedal.

On a road bike, however, when everyone is using the same size wheel and the sprockets all fall within a certain range, it is more usual just to declare two numbers, as in 'Pushing a 53/12', which is enough to impress anybody (53 teeth on your chainring, 12 on your sprocket).

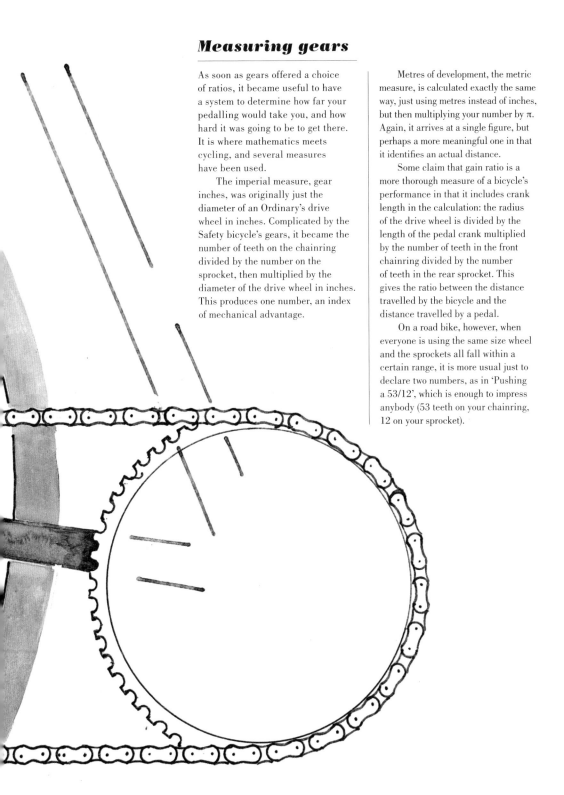

Oscar Egg, 1934. Brooks saddle, everything else Egg. As well as devising the most effective and successful drive train of his era, Egg manufactured frames.

Clanger

All the early work seemed to go towards devising a workable rear derailleur, and it was only later that a pair of chainrings were fitted to offer more ratios.

First, in the late 1940s, a fork-shaped guide pushed the chain sideways, deflecting it from one chainring to the next, operated with a lever mounted on the seat tube. These were known as 'clangers' for obvious reasons. A cable-operated front changer became standard in 1960.

The most radical change in derailleurs since the 1960s has been the introduction of electronic shifting: a set of gears and tiny motors replace the usual cables that pull against springs to move the derailleur. Electronic gears are lighter, more accurate and faster than cable systems. First developed in the 1990s, electronic shifting made a couple of false starts before becoming reliable enough to be viable, but by 2009 it was common in the professional peloton.

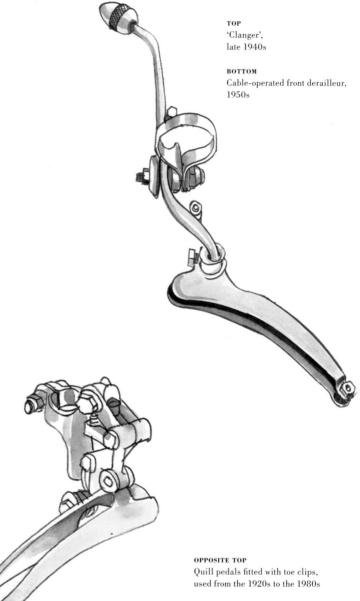

TOP
'Clanger',
late 1940s

BOTTOM
Cable-operated front derailleur,
1950s

OPPOSITE TOP
Quill pedals fitted with toe clips,
used from the 1920s to the 1980s

OPPOSITE MIDDLE
Cinelli's innovative M71:
the notorious 'death cleats',
1971

OPPOSITE BOTTOM
LOOK ski-boot-inspired effective
solution, 1984

Pedals

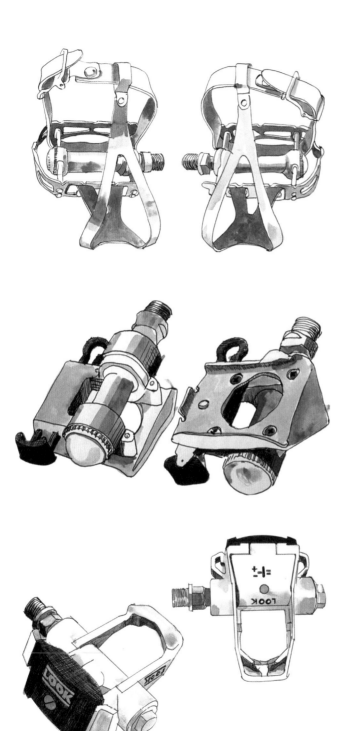

The first contact point devised to link the foot to a drive was a treadle, similar to the ones used on a loom: rods converted vertical movement into rotation. Pedals themselves began as simple platforms – first wooden blocks, then metal, then rubber, before going back to metal, and now, inevitably, carbon. Bearings eliminated friction between the pedal and its axle.

Quill pedals were developed for racing, the platform being reduced to a minimal metal frame. Toe clips, metal cages with binding straps, allowed the pedals to be pulled up as well as pushed down, increasing the powered part of the rotation. To further engage the shoe with the pedal a slotted metal plate – a nail – was sometimes attached to the shoe, engaging with a matching ridge on the pedal. These improved efficiency, but were hard to release. The arrival of an effective lipless pedal rendered the quill pedal obsolete in the mid-1980s.

Confusingly, pedals that are clipped into are called clipless. A cleat fixed under the shoe engages with a spring-loaded mechanism in the pedal, fixing the foot firmly to the drive. The first clipless pedal was invented by Charles Hanson in 1895. In 1971 Cinelli introduced its M71 pedal. To disengage, the rider had to reach down to operate a release. They quickly earned the name 'death cleats'.

Not until 1984 did LOOK, the French manufacturer of ski bindings, introduce a cleat that disengaged by simply twisting the foot. Promoted by Bernard Hinault, they quickly became standard. Numerous patterns of pedal and cleat have been devised, aiming to provide a stable and efficient platform. It is the cleats on their stiff shoes that account for the awkward clattering gait of cyclists walking to their bikes.

Handlebars

The first steerable bikes used a simple wooden handle on each side of the front fork to turn them. As metal took over, bars were first narrow and straight on the boneshakers and Ordinaries but quickly widened as the advantage of having some leverage in steering became obvious. Longer and sweeping backwards on the Safety, they then curved downwards to arrive at the familiar drop-bar profile by the early 1910s. Drop bars offer a choice of riding positions and their ergonomics can be carefully controlled through subtle variations in their curves and dimensions.

Handlebars were always made from steel, the only material thought to be strong enough, until Cinelli introduced their first aluminium bars in 1964. After that, Italian handlebars steered every racing bike until carbon became strong enough to take over. In the 1980s the clip-on aero bar appeared in time trial stages, as

advantages were sought in aerodynamics: the rider stretched out to reach the extensions, crouching into a tucked position, with elbows supported by pads on the bars. Along with a smoothly profiled helmet, aero bars were held to be responsible for the eight seconds that won Greg LeMond the 1989 Tour de France. Ever since though, the UCI seems to have had an ambivalent attitude to them, writing into race regulations minutely detailed constraints on their dimensions and the exact posture that they impose on the rider. Doubts have been raised about their safety in anything but time

trials, as they take a rider's hands away from the brakes, and deliver questionable stability. Since 2000, bars have inevitably been made from carbon fibre, in painstakingly tunnel-tested aerodynamic profiles.

In the 1990s Francesco Moser, Graeme Obree and Chris Boardman juggled the World Hour Record between them on a succession of unconventionally configured bicycles where innovative handlebars contrived increasingly extreme riding positions. These were usually outlawed by the UCI as soon as they proved to be successful.

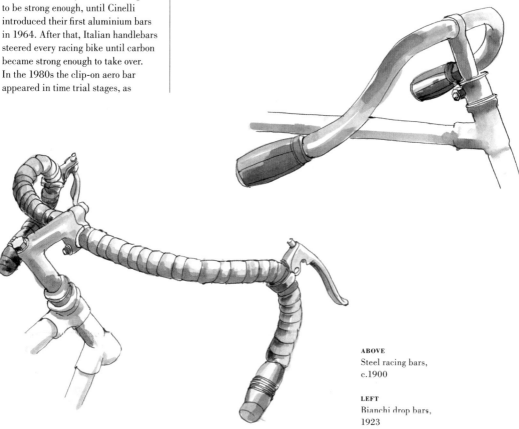

ABOVE
Steel racing bars,
c.1900

LEFT
Bianchi drop bars,
1923

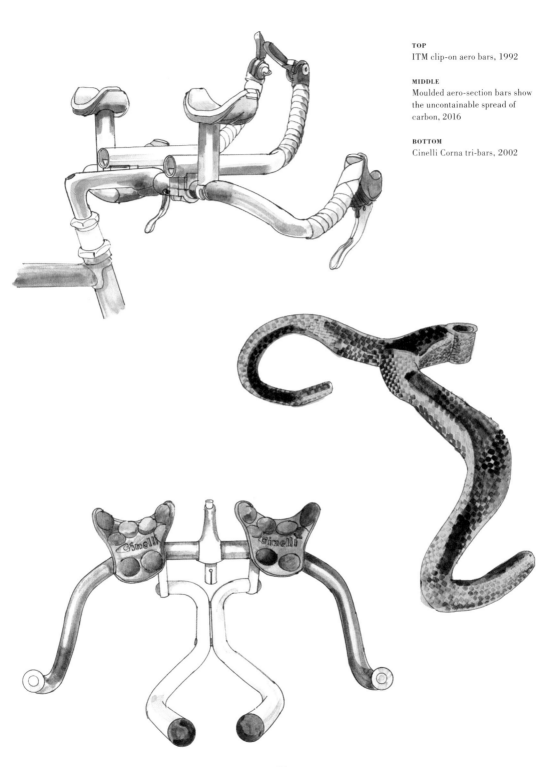

Bottecchia, as raced on the Champs-Élysées by Greg LeMond to gain his eight-second victory, 1989.

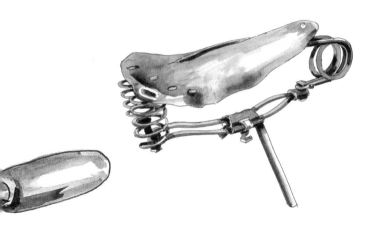

Saddles

The seats on the first Draisiennes clearly revealed their pedigree: they were obviously taken straight from the back of a pony. More suitable saddles were quickly developed, some with large springs, which were essential before the introduction of the pneumatic tyre.

As tyres softened the ride, the seat could be slimmed down, and soon saddles were no more than a leather cover stretched over metal rails. Leather, though, required careful maintenance, as it took up water in the rain and set like stone as it dried out. In 1970 the Cinelli Unicanitor, the first plastic-shelled saddle, was introduced. It was both lighter and more stable than leather. Springs were long gone and the rails slimmed down, and from then on it was the by now familiar story of reducing and lightening to find the most minimal yet viable support to race on, followed by the eventual arrival of carbon for the shell and the rails.

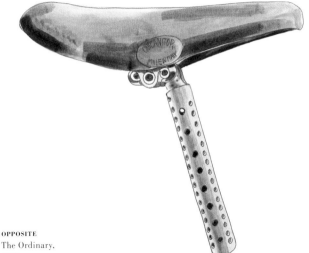

OPPOSITE
The Ordinary,
1870s

TOP
James Starley's Safety bicycle,
1884. Leather mounted on large
steel springs.

MIDDLE
Cinelli Unicanitor, the first
synthetic saddle, 1970.
This one is mounted on a
drillium seat post.

BOTTOM
Moulded cover and rails, 2016.
Carbon spreads to the saddle.

Brakes

It is expedient to have a way of making a bicycle stop, or at least slow down, a fact recognized by Karl Drais, who had already in 1818 contrived a brake on his Draisienne.

The first brakes were crude paddles pressed onto the solid tyre, known as 'spoon brakes'. Wooden wheels were too fragile to be used as a braking surface. The Duck brake of 1897, made by the American Abraham Duck, applied a pair of friction rollers to the tyre, a lever augmenting the force applied – with both hands if necessary.

As rims were made stronger they were able to act as the braking surface. Early rim brakes pressed upwards against the inside of the wheel and were activated by rods.

Devised in 1887, caliper brakes pivot above the wheel, activated by cables pulling on the two extended arms of each side. The pads press onto each side of the wheel rim. This arrangement, improved by a second pivot, has long been the standard for road bikes. One notable exception, however, was the Campagnolo Record brakeset introduced in the mid-1980s. An ergonomic triangular faceplate enclosed a parallelogram of eight linkages that articulated under pressure to apply the brake. Though one of the most beautiful components ever offered, its performance is acknowledged to be unimpressive.

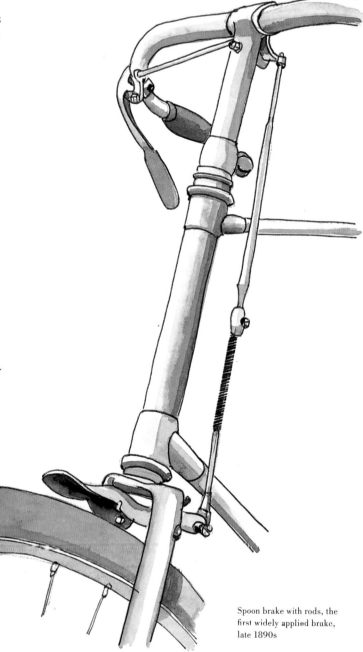

Spoon brake with rods, the first widely applied brake, late 1890s

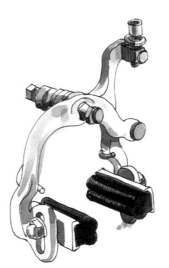

RIGHT
Caliper brakes, invented 1887.
Cork or felt pads protect delicate
wooden rims.

BELOW
Campagnolo Super Record
caliper brakes, 1974

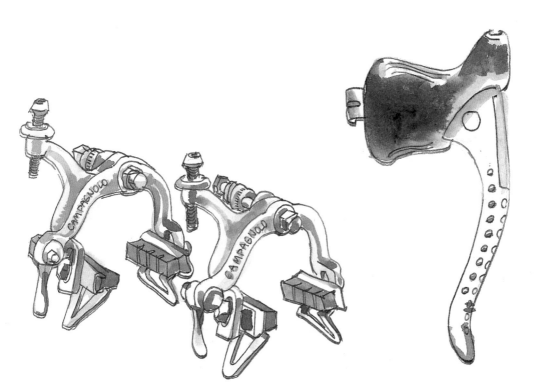

Drillium brake lever, a weight-
saving modification widespread
in the 1970s

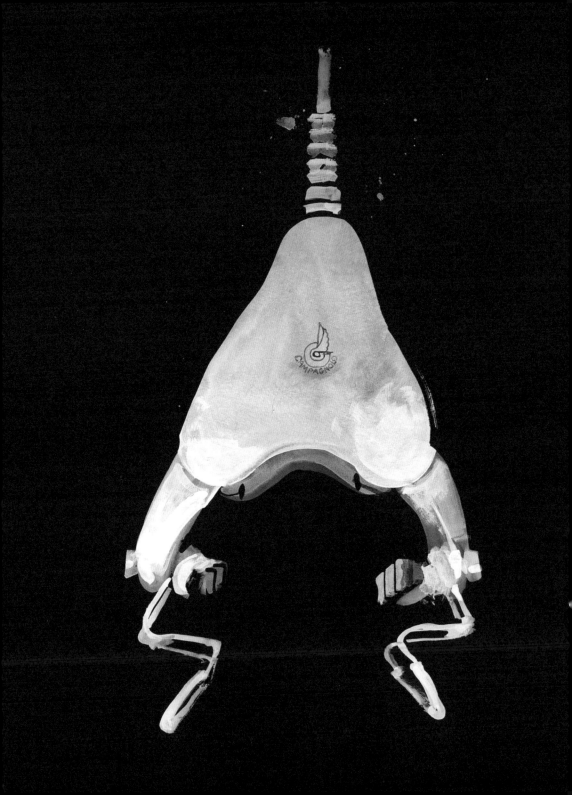

Disc brakes

The rim brake is light and efficient, but it is drastically compromised in wet conditions and grinds the rim with road-dirt. Disc brakes, however, use pads that close on a rotor mounted on one side of the hub. More efficient in braking power than rim brakes, and less affected by the weather, they are standard on mountain bikes. But there are problems. Brakes work by turning kinetic energy into heat. The smaller braking surface of disc brakes is liable to overheat: brake fluid has been known to boil on long descents. Braking action being applied to just one side of the wheel at the hub transfers its forces through the whole wheel to the tyre asymmetrically. This has consequences for both hub and wheel construction. There is also a suspicion that the turning rotor has the potential to deliver severe wounds in a pile-up: injuries have been carefully examined for the marks of disc-brake rotors to determine if they were at fault. It has also been suggested that riders using different braking systems in the same peloton will result in more crashes.

OPPOSITE AND ABOVE
Campagnolo Record Delta, 1984. One of the most elegant components ever manufactured.

RIGHT
Disc brake, still under scrutiny at the time of writing.

Races

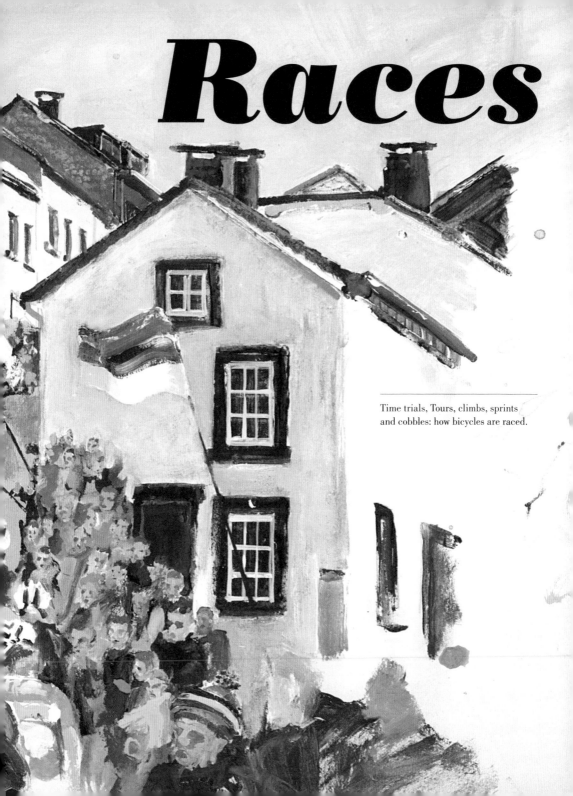

Time trials, Tours, climbs, sprints
and cobbles: how bicycles are raced.

How Races Are Run

In the early days cycle races were run on a track, or across huge distances between European cities. Cycle racing evolved in different disciplines and specialisms: track and road; one-day and stage races; criterium; massed start; time trials; team races.

A stage race is a race of stages – *étapes* – with each day of racing adding to the total time. Whoever has the lowest cumulative time is the leader of the General Classification, or GC (CG in France), and the overall leader of the race. It is quite usual to win the race without ever winning a stage.

In addition to the GC there are several other categories. High finishes both at the end of the race and at designated segments of the route contribute to a points jersey, effectively for the most consistent sprinter. The King of the Mountains is self-explanatory. There also awards for best young rider and most combative rider, and there is even said to be a best-dressed rider

category on the Giro. For a time the Giro also offered a jersey, the *maglia nera*, for the rider in last place, but this was withdrawn when it was seen to promote the wrong attitude to racing at the back of the field.

Flat finishes favour group riding as they usually end in a sprint finish in which thoroughly drilled teams work to bring their star sprinter to the front, aiming to time their manoeuvre to allow him to reserve his effort for the last few metres. This is the sprint train, perfected for Mario Cipollini in the 1980s.

Mountains reward the individual, with the strongest climber casting off the rest of the peloton in a process of attrition.

In time trials riders race against the clock (*contre le montre*) in rigidly enforced individual stages where team support cannot help. There is no one to keep you out of the wind, and no one will bring you a bottle. A time trial can be on the flat or on a mountain.

Sprinting

Heavily muscled sprinters can deliver the huge surge of power needed to win in the last 50 metres, but they rely on being brought to the front by a dedicated sprint train. The craft of sprinting lies in doing it across the shortest possible distance and getting the timing just right – an attack that comes too early is always swallowed up. Their muscle weighs heavily in the mountains, where, if they have not already gone home, the sprinters usually form themselves into an *autobus*, a confederation that ensures they all avoid elimination.

Flat stage finishes are the domain of the sprinters. Whatever happens in the countless preceding kilometres, it is the final 100 metres where the race happens. Lead-out men carve a path through the peloton to deliver their sprinter to the front, to launch his attack at the latest possible opportunity. Dozens of riders will be racing flat out, shoulder to shoulder at 60km/h (37mph). Elbows, shoulders and headbutts are commonly used to carve out a path, inevitably leading to spectacular crashes. The peloton's cumulative momentum regularly devastates whole swathes of riders.

Climbing

That races are won in the mountains is a widely repeated cliché. While a time trial might offer up an advantage of a few seconds, a day in the mountains might put 10 minutes between riders. Whole *gruppettos* can fall so far behind that they are disqualified. Sprinters suffer horribly as they have to carry their muscle over the mountains, while the lightly built climbers fight it out in front of them. Dense crowds of hysterical fans line the roads with camper-vans, hurling water and chasing bikes, making a frenzied corridor for the riders to pass through. The classic climbs witness scenes of grotesque fancy dress, and riders are forced to dodge giant rubber hands, running fans and thoughtfully squirted bidons of water and other liquids.

Before gears were introduced, it was impossible to ride many of the mountain passes, and riders pushed their bikes over the worst of the climbs.

Elimination

Individuals, or even whole groups, can be eliminated from the race if on any stage they drop too far behind. This is measured as a percentage of the stage winner's time, and can vary from 104 per cent on an easy stage, to a margin of 25 per cent on a severe mountain stage, leading to some mental arithmetic at the back of the field, as the *autobus* works out how fast it needs to travel.

Time trials

Time trialling tests individual strength and endurance. There is no pace line to let you recover at the back, and no one in front to keep you out of the wind. Courses can be long, short, flat or steep. Strict distance is enforced between competitors: you really are on your own. At some point you have to come out from behind your domestiques if you are going to win a race...

Marco Pantani in the *maglia rosa* during the 1998 Giro d'Italia.

Alcyon (badged *L'Auto*), 1930. This bicycle was issued to all riders in the Tour de France in an attempt to measure the man and not the machine.

Tour de France

First route

Created by Henri Desgrange as a publicity stunt for his newspaper, *L'Auto*, the Tour de France is the best race in the world, a seething spectacle of competition and drama, physical performance and human nature. Every year, for three weeks in July, millions of people are gripped by the spectacle of 200 men in garishly branded lycra racing through France and its neighbours, day after day, over the Alps and Pyrenees, towards the Grande Arrivée on the Champs-Élysées.

The original Tour, the model for every stage race that followed, was conceived from a combination of commerce, politics and ambition. The Dreyfus Affair, France's all-enveloping political scandal, lasting more than 20 years, caused, among its other effects, a rift in sports publishing. In the resulting bitter rivalry between the established *Le Vélo*, and its upstart rival, the yellow-paged *L'Auto*, editor Henri Desgrange knew a good idea when it was brought to him, and the notion of a tour of France became a reality in 1903 when *L'Auto* launched the first 'edition' of the race.

The first race covered nearly 2,500km (1,550mi) in six massive stages and was won by Maurice Garin in 93 hours. This was the beginning of a complex canon of statistics and records that the race generates for its devotees to speculate and obsess over. The hard facts of time and distance, though, can never explain the Tour, also known as La Grande Boucle (The Great Loop), as they are complicated by a code of practice and customs of racing that contrive a far more sophisticated narrative than can the bare metrics of comparative performances. Immediately successful, it has gone on to be a competition like no other sporting event, an irresistible spectacle of physical endurance and personal drama combined with an intriguing complexity of race regulations, codes and customs, with a significant contribution from the hand of random fate.

From the very start, cheating, sabotage and copious consumption of stimulants were all part of the race. It nearly failed to survive its second year, after descending into a chaos of cheating and crowd violence. The

race included night stages at this time, and under cover of darkness extreme liberties were taken. The success of the first race had drawn large crowds, who participated enthusiastically, assaulting some riders and sabotaging others. Twice order could only be restored with gunshots. Riders took shortcuts, rode on trains and in cars, and even arranged to be towed, holding a cork in their teeth, connected to a car with a cord. Sundry infringements incurred penalties or physical attacks, and Desgrange despaired that the anarchy of 1904 would spell the end of his big idea. In later races, a system of unannounced checkpoints was installed on the route, at least one on every stage. Riders would be rubber-stamped on their hand as they passed through, evidence of conformity to the route that would be demanded at the finish.

Early editions of the Tour were strictly individual affairs. For Desgrange, the perfect race would eliminate everyone but the last rider left in the saddle. Individual heroism was his mantra, and the early editions were strictly regulated, banning any kind of outside assistance, mechanical or strategic.

In 1913, Eugène Christophe received a 10-minute penalty when,

Henri Desgrange

- 52 -

The epitome of spectacle: Marco Pantani in the Alps.

Alpe d'Huez

This is the movie star of the mountains. With 21 hairpin bends and 1,072 metres (3,500 feet) of climb, Alpe d'Huez has become the first among giants. It was first climbed by the Tour de France in 1952, when Fausto Coppi beat Jean Robic to the top. Marco Pantani holds the record for the fastest ascent, at 37' 35" (Miguel Induráin is the fastest untainted by drugs, at 39' 28" in 1995). In 2013 riders rode up the Alpe, down the Alpe and then back up the Alpe again. Due to its invariable occupation by thousands of fans from the Netherlands, it is, paradoxically, referred to as 'The Dutch Mountain'. Riders proceed up the mountain in an increasingly narrow channel between hoards of hysterical and erratic fans who camp out on the road for days, a rowdy caravan stretching up the mountain.

Successive corners have been named after the winners of the stage, though, having been raced more than 21 times, this system is now somewhat confused.

Maurice Brocco, the bête noir of Desgrange.

after having walked in tears down the Tourmalet with broken forks, he found a forge and set about fixing them in the furnace. A small boy pumped the bellows and this was judged to be 'assistance', earning the penalty that lost the race for Christophe, who never placed better than third.

The obsession with individual effort was eventually challenged when the role of domestique was unilaterally introduced by the riders. 'Domestique!' was the insult *L'Auto* hurled at Maurice Brocco, a promising rider who in 1911 arranged – for a fee – to pace François Faber for a day in the Pyrenees. An outraged Desgrange stopped short of disqualifying Brocco, but used his newspaper to vent his disgust. The following day Brocco rode away with the race over the Aubisque and the Tourmalet, taunting Desgrange with his tactical manipulations.

The function of domestique swiftly became firmly established, and the form of the stage race was changed. A team structure, in which the star is supported and protected by a closely controlled squad of subordinate riders, became the model. Trade teams were assembled by bicycle manufacturers, such as Alcyon, Elvish and Mercier.

In 1930 Desgrange reorganized the race into national and regional teams, to rid the Tour of the trade teams he so despised. It was still a

Mont Ventoux

Length 21.4km (13.29mi)	
Average gradient 7.6%	
Maximum gradient 12%	
Elevation gain 1,639m (5,377ft)	

'A God of Evil ... a higher hell', is how Roland Barthes described Mont Ventoux, perhaps over-egging it a bit. An isolated mountain rising up from the surrounding plains, its photogenic qualities as well as the physical challenge it presents ensure its iconic status.

Invariably described as being like the moon, Mont Ventoux is baked by the sun and scoured by the winds, its last kilometres above the tree line bare and white, stripped by the shipbuilders of Toulon. Halfway up, riders pass the memorial to Tommy Simpson, the British rider who succumbed to the heat in 1967. The contribution of his drug intake to his death is still subject to debate. Contrary to popular belief his last words were not 'Put me back on my bike!' but 'On, on, on!' A testing place for heroes, including Eddy Merckx, who needed oxygen when he reached the summit in the 1970 Tour de France. The fastest ascent is by Iban Mayo in 2004, in 55' 51".

Maillots (FR)

To distinguish who is leading which category within the melee of garishly clad riders, race leaders are awarded colour-coded jerseys, or *maillots*. The first marker for a race leader was a green armband, worn on the early editions of the Tour de France. The arrival of the *maillot jaune* (yellow jersey) for the leader of the General Classification (GC) for the Tour de France is hard to date, and black-and-white photography is unable to help. The Belgian Philippe Thys seemed to remember being awarded one in 1913, but the first GC leader in yellow is more usually accepted as having been Eugène Christophe in 1919. It was not until 1987 that the *maillot jaune* was complemented with a stuffed toy lion, courtesy of sponsor Credit Lyonnais. There was some resistance to the choice of colour of the leader's jersey at first, and the reason for its selection is again disputed. It might have represented the yellow pages of *L'Auto*, but it is also suggested that yellow shirts were cheaper due to their unpopularity.

While plain colours served to identify the points and young rider categories (green and white respectively), the King of the Mountains has since 1975 been identified by the exotic red-on-white polka-dot jersey. Widely believed to represent the livery of a chocolate maker, the *maillot à pois* (jersey with peas) was in fact devised by French rider Henri Lemoine in the 1930s, inspired by the silks of jockeys. Félix Lévitan, co-directeur of the Tour, and fan of 'Le P'tit Pois', as Lemoine was known, had the design copied for the King of the Mountains jersey, and its success inspired sponsors Chocolat Poulain to adopt the pattern as well.

The first man to wear the *maillot à pois*, Belgian Lucien Van Impe, is reported to have complained that he looked like a clown, which was true, but that did not stop the polka dot from going on to become the mark of the climber in many international stage races.

A combativity category has been awarded since 1953, promoted to 'super-combativity' in 2003. Now recognized only by a white number on a red background, for a time it had its own jersey, a melange of all the other jerseys. This has now been abandoned, perhaps on aesthetic grounds...

a distressed state by a search party at 3 o'clock the following morning. Revived, he disingenuously telegraphed his boss:

Crossed Tourmalet … Stop
Very Good Road … Stop
Perfectly Passable … Stop
… *Steinès*.

So the scene was set for the 'Tour of the Assassins' in 1910. Not content with the 1,400m (4,600ft) of climbing the Tourmalet demanded, three other major cols were added to make a 300km (186mi) stage like none that had ever been attempted before. Roads were unsealed cart tracks, bikes were single speed and weighed more than 12kg (26lb), and the route offered over 9,000m (29,500ft) of climbing.

First over the Aubisque was François Lafourcade, pushing his bike. Fifteen minutes later Octave Lapize appeared. *L'Auto*'s marshals were there, keenly observing the effect of their first venture in the mountains. As he passed, Lapize gasped, '*Vous êtes des assassins! Oui, des assassins.*'

Only one rider – Gustave Garrigou – crossed the Tourmalet still riding his bike, for which he received a 100 franc bonus. The stage was judged a great success and Desgrange believed his Tour was now complete, having been tested against the most severe terrain.

The mountains continue to offer the greatest spectacle: the most vivid suffering against the most picturesque backdrops. Variations on the Circle of Death regularly appear, though now the stage is unlikely to be much more than 170km (105mi), with 5,000m (16,400ft) of climbing, bikes that struggle to keep to the 6.8kg (15lb) minimum weight, and sealed roads. Offsetting these advantages, though, contemporary riders have to climb through a narrow path between thousands of hysterical fans desperate to participate by stripping to their mankinis, putting on onesies, hurling water, letting off smoke bombs, capturing selfies and running alongside riders offering advice.

The Circle of Death

Col d'Aubisque, Col du Tourmalet, Col d'Aspin and Col de Peyresourde: these hills make up the Circle of Death, though it's not really a circle, and no one has died racing on them. But the dawn of racing in big mountains broke in the Pyrenees, over the Tourmalet and its monumental neighbours. It's the heartland of Grand Tour superlatives, both in words and on the bike.

Henri Desgrange, always open to ways of making his race harder, sent his aide Alphonse Steinès to reconnoitre the highest pass in the Pyrenees. In January. Setting out with a companion who soon turned back, fearing bears, Steinès abandoned his car and managed to struggle over the pass, only to be found in

team race, but now every rider would compete for his country, on a standardized yellow bike supplied by *L'Auto*. To fund this de-commercialized Tour, the 'Caravane Publicitaire' was conceived: sponsors paid to send advertising vehicles out as part of the Tour spectacle. So began the caravan, a cavalcade of increasingly exhibitionist vehicles sent out before the race. Giant cheeses, beer bottles, vacuum cleaners, 2CVs dressed in gingham, wine bottles and enormous lions have all appeared, with blaring klaxons and grinning crews, showering the crowds with ephemera en route. The caravan is perhaps epitomized by the sombrero-sporting queen of the accordion, Yvette Horner, playing *chansons* from the roof of a liveried Citroën Traction Avant;

she participated in 11 consecutive Tours between 1952 and 1963. The Tour now travels everywhere with its caravan, even if that means shipping dozens of funny cars to England for three days, as they did in 2014. The caravan, however, is now widely criticized for the lamentable quality of the souvenirs hurled to the crowd, and the disco-blaring procession of floats flogging a banal series of products is now a grimily vulgar commercial version of its former charming self. Opinion is also divided over the quality of public support on the roadside, as a hysterical and well-refreshed mob of exhibitionists fight for media coverage in a garish uniform of mankinis, fright wigs and cheap fancy dress.

For ten years the peloton rode yellow bicycles (mostly made by Alcyon) badged with *L'Auto* and wore jerseys in national colours. After World War II individual manufacturers returned and a bit of discreet branding reappeared on chests and legs.

National teams continued until 1962, when the needs of the financially squeezed manufacturers prevailed and teams were again organized around commercial sponsors, and the deluge of branding was launched.

Champs-Élysées

It seems inevitable that the Tour should finish on the most celebrated boulevard of the world's most romantic city, but the Grande Arrivée has only been located on the Champs-Élysées since 1975. Before that the race ended in suburban velodromes, first the Parc des Princes, and then at Vincennes.

The Champs-Élysées is usually the end of a largely ceremonial stage for the GC leader – it is an informal convention that the yellow jersey will not be challenged on the final day – so the finish has become a sprinter's showcase. Eight circuits of the Arc de Triomphe end in a fiercely contested mass finish, with the strong possibility of catastrophic accidents adding a frisson to the spectacle. Mark Cavendish might have the best record on the Champs-Élysées, but the most remembered event on the boulevard is probably Djamolidine Abdoujaparov's explosive wipeout in 1991, closely followed by Wilfried Nelissen's disastrous encounter with a policeman in 1994.

Kisses, suntans and soft toys mark the Grande Arrivée of the Tour de France on the Champs-Élysées.

The distinctive orange Merckx Molteni bike of 1972.

Giro d'Italia

First route

Six years younger than the Tour, the Giro is Italy's great race. Like the Tour, it was established as a promotional tool for a newspaper, Milan's *Gazzetta dello Sport*, and it similarly took an immediate hold on the imagination of the country. (The episodic nature of the stage races made them ideal lures to bait newspaper buyers.) Based in Milan, the race both started and finished there for the first three years until 1911.

Characterized by enormous stage lengths and vast mountain climbs, the early race was run over unsealed roads on heavy single-speed bicycles. Endemic cheating, devious chicanery and dubious tactical scheming combined with political and commercial manipulation often made the early years of the race dramatic for all the wrong reasons. The 1948 race nearly collapsed as half the field retired in disgust after Fiorenzo Magni was pushed over the Passo Pordoi, passed from one helping hand to the next by a chain of supporters, allegedly bussed in to help by his Wilier Triestina team.

Very much a national race, it was 1950 before a non-Italian, the Swiss Hugo Koblet, won the Giro. Statistically the Italians have kept a tighter grip on it than the French have the Tour: nearly 70 per cent of Giros have been won by a home rider, while only a third of Tours have seen French success (half of the Vueltas have been won by Spaniards).

Being run at the end of May, and taking in the highest of Itay's mountain passes, the Giro is vulnerable to extremes of weather, but its organizers have seemed happy to turn a blind eye to spectacularly unsuitable conditions. This has spawned some legendary battles against the elements: Monte Bondone in 1956, the Stelvio pass in 1965 and the Gavia pass in 1988 were all epic feats of endurance. The peloton can regularly be seen passing through deep cuttings of snow, in weather completely unsuitable for bicycle racing. In 1988 Andy Hampsten, engulfed in a blizzard over the Gavia, adopted skiing kit on his way to winning the race.

The Giro's first winner was Luigi Ganna, in 1909, after which

Passo Stelvio

Length 24.3km (15mi)

Average gradient 7.4%

Maximum gradient 11%

Elevation gain 1,808m (5,932ft)

A spectacular looping set of 48 hairpins draped up the side of the valley, at 2,757m (9,045ft) the Stelvio is the highest col on any Grand Tour route. It is the apex of the Giro, and scene of Fausto Coppi's triumphant annihilation of Hugo Koblet, and everyone else, in 1953.

The Cima Coppi (literally, 'the top') is the name given to the highest pass on each year's Giro, but the Stelvio is the original and iconic Cima Coppi.

The Giro, the first Grand Tour of the year, often encounters extreme conditions when it reaches the mountains.

the race was dominated by Alfredo Binda between 1925 and 1929, to the point where the inevitability of his winning turned the fans against him. To encourage the others he was induced not to compete in 1930 and to ride the Tour de France instead, but he mysteriously abandoned the race after winning two stages. Non-payment of his financial inducement was later identified as the cause of his retirement.

In 1931 both Binda and his challenger, the young and enormously popular Learco Guerra, fell victim to the *maledizione della maglia rosa* (curse of the pink jersey): Binda crashed out, while Guerra was knocked off his bike by an over-enthusiastic supporter.

The classic years of the Giro were between 1935 and 1953, when Fausto Coppi and Gino Bartali duelled for the *maglia rosa*. Gino the Pious, the darling of the Vatican and conservative Italy, against Fausto, the new arrogant

and ultimately unstoppable force. Coppi is widely held to be the greatest cyclist ever, and the 1949 Giro his definitive performance. Ultimately it was Coppi who triumphed, winning five Giros to Bartali's three.

The next rider to conclusively dominate the Giro was Eddie Merckx, 'the Cannibal'. Merckx arrived at the Giro considered a sprinter, but proceeded to annihilate the competition in all areas, outclimbing in the mountains as well as winning the sprints.

Passo Gavia

Length 17.3km (10.75mi)

Average gradient 7.4%

Maximum gradient 16%

Elevation gain 1,363m (4,472ft)

Mostly unsealed, the Gavia pass has been the scene of some of the most extreme Grand Tour racing ever seen. Often hosting the Giro in late May – when snow, frequently turning to ice, is usual, and delivered in blizzards – it regularly provides conditions that test the viability of riding mountain stages in anything but high summer. In 1965 riders carried their bikes through head-high drifts, and in 1988 Erik Breukink and Andy Hampsten led an epic crossing of the pass, in what appeared to be Arctic conditions, as a decimated field in improvised winter clothing struggled to follow.

Costante Girardengo and Alfredo Binda, 1925

Marco Pantani

Maglias (IT)

While the Tour has *maillots*, the Giro has *maglias*. Depite Benito Mussolini's reluctance, a pink jersey, the *maglia rosa*, was adopted in 1931 for the overall leader. This was immediately accessorized by the *maledizione della maglia rosa* (curse of the pink jersey), as successive incumbents succumbed to disasters en route.

The *maglia ciclamino/rosso* (or cyclamen/red jersey) is for points and the *verde/azzura* (green/sky blue) for climbing. For six years in the 1940s the Giro awarded a *maglia nera* (black jersey) for the last-placed rider, formalizing the unofficial *lanterne rouge* that had been initiated on the Tour de France. Competition for the jersey was keen, and riders in contention made committed attempts to lose time by meandering, lingering, hiding and even sabotaging their own bikes to ensure a low placing – but not so low as to be eliminated, which was the art of achieving the *maglia nera*. The *maglia* was withdrawn after the 1951 race, the spectacle of trying to lose being considered undignified.

Vuelta a España

First route

Maillots (ES)

The Vuelta, a bit younger, and with a less consistent history than the other two tours, has awarded a confusing variety of *maillots*.

A *maillot oro* (gold) was the first choice for GC leader, which changed to white for a year before reverting. Then for five years it was white with a red band. For the next thirty years, apart from a brief return to gold, it was yellow, then gold again for ten, before a red jersey was debuted in 2010.

The King of the Mountains shirt was first green, then a polka dot (but white on red, the reverse of the French version), though for a while in the 1980s sponsorship transformed it into 'coffee beans on white'. A brief spell as plain orange followed, before it became the *maillot lunares azules* (blue polka-dot jersey) in 2010.

The points jersey is now green, but, like the mountain *maillot*, a previous sponsorship deal asserted its branding for a time, making it blue with yellow fish on it.

Other tours arrange their own jersey codes, but often borrow from the Grand Tours: the Tour of California has a yellow GC jersey with a bear featured on it; the Tour of Oman red, like the Vuelta; the Tour of Britain yellow again.

Madrid's *Informaciones* is the journal that conceived the last of the three Grand Tours, but the Vuelta was born out of political and nationalist ambitions, rather than commercial. The Gran Premio República was a stage race inaugurated in 1932 to celebrate the arrival of democracy in Spain following the departure of King Alfonso XIII. The race was intended to help build the notion of a unified country. In 1935 *Informaciones* expanded on the idea of the Gran Premio (GP) to create the Vuelta a España, an ambitious national Grand Tour. The short-lived Republic was, however, violently replaced by General Francisco Franco's fascist regime. While the politics had changed, the race was still just as useful to a dictator stamping his face on a country, so, after a four-year hiatus during hostilities, it returned in 1941.

Spain's Grand Tour closely follows the model of the other two: a three-week stage race describing the shape of the country but open to excursions abroad for the right incentives. Though it was largely a domestic event for much of its early life, the first two Vueltas were won by a Belgian, Gustaaf Deloor. The first Spanish winner was Julián Berrendero in 1941, winner of the GP República and the King of the Mountains at the Tour de France in 1936. He had, though, ridden as a Republican, and before he could compete in Franco's Spain he spent 18 months in a concentration camp. Berrendero won two Vueltas before it was again suspended during World War II. The race has remained a fiercely protested political symbol, though, as its assertion of a monolithic Spain is challenged to this day by separatists: nails, oil slicks and bombs have met the race in the Basque country, culminating in a particularly violent year in 1977. After that the race avoided the region for over 30 years. Partial political autonomy, its own UCI-ranked tour, and a Basque-recruited and -funded team – Euskaltel–Euskadi – have brought a calmer atmosphere to both the region and the race. This has allowed the Vuelta to secure its international status, thus completing the pyramid of the three Grand Tours.

Originally run in the spring, it was moved in 1995 to September to avoid a clash with the Giro.

The Vuelta displays the distinctive landscapes of Spain just as the other two Grand Tours display their great national landscapes.

The Five Monuments

Bicycle racing was born in Europe at the end of the nineteenth century. Some road races have persisted across the decades, surviving as the Classics. Up to 30 races claim Classic status, though their significance, venerability and reputation is open to debate – and vulnerable to the whim of organizing bodies. The five most revered of these have become known collectively as the Monuments to distinguish them from the more contentious candidates.

Milan–San Remo
1907

Held in March, this is the first race of the season, earning the nickname 'La Primavera' (Spring) or 'La Classicissima'. First run in 1907, it is a flat race across northern Italy, and the longest of the Classics at nearly 300km (186mi). Several climbs are featured on the race, but it ends in a sprinter's finish on the chic Via Roma in San Remo. It is the race every Italian wants to win: Merckx achieved 7 wins, but the race belongs to Costante Girardengo, with 11 podium finishes and 6 first places.

Ronde van Vlaanderen
1913

The Ronde van Vlaanderen (Tour of Flanders), run in April, is known as 'Vlaanderens Mooiste', or 'Flanders' Finest'. Founded in 1913, it is Belgium's biggest bike race and notorious for its brutal climbs up cobbled gullies. Along with another Monument, Paris–Roubaix, it is one of the four spring races that make up the Cobbled Classics, which are physically demanding in ways unlike any other races: the climbs might be much shorter than the big mountains, but their cobbled surfaces sabotage randomly and once you are off, there is no getting back on, with the peloton filling the trench you were trying to ride up. (Racing conditions are regularly appalling.)

Out of the mass of statistics built up over hundreds of races, it is notable that only Belgians have won all five Monuments: Rik Van Looy, Roger De Vlaeminck and, inevitably, Eddy Merckx, with 8, 11 and 19 wins respectively.

Cobbles

The fields of northern France and Belgium make a dour backdrop compared to the picturesque spectacle of racing past Mediterranean, Alpine and Pyrenean vistas: flat farmland more likely to feature potatoes than sunflowers, leaden skies, mud or dust. Not surprisingly the region is celebrated for a style of cycling built around heroic endurance in the face of persistent punishment. Here, perseverance pays off as often as inspiration.

The rolling courses of the Flandrien Classics are punctuated by brutal climbs – not long like the great mountains, but punishingly steep, with treacherous surfaces ramping up through claustrophobic trenches lined with enthusiasts sustained by Belgium's other great export. The melee of cyclists, outriders and team cars pour up the gullies in a chaotic chase always seemingly poised on the edge of disaster. Here road racing meets cyclocross, and it is usual to see a lot of bikes being carried up the climbs.

In the brutal climbs of Northern European Classics, paved gulleys confront the peloton.

The legendary *pavé*, now meticulously preserved to maintain the tradition of suffering.

Paris–Roubaix
1896

The most controversial of all the Classics, Paris–Roubaix is a unique mix of competition and folly. It has been described as 'bullshit' by Bernard Hinault (the 1981 winner), and 'a circus' by Chris Boardman, who never entered.

The race is one of the Cobbled Classics, conceived when the cobble (or sett, a quarried rectangular stone) was the usual construction of northern European roads. These tortuous surfaces are now lovingly maintained by enthusiasts – Les Forçats du Pavé (Convicts of the Pavement) – to ensure the races retain their characteristic agony. First run in 1896, the brainchild of two Roubaix textile manufacturers to promote their velodrome, the race was always intended to be tough. The stone *pavés* add a whole other dimension of difficulty, discomfort and potential disaster to the race, and the 'Queen of the Classics', as it is known, tests riders and bicycles in cruel and unusual ways. Teams constantly try to supply equipment that will be competitive while taking some of the pain out of racing over large cobblestones. Padding, suspension, fat tyres and extra brake levers have all been tried.

Run in April, the weather and the surface conspire to produce conditions totally unsuitable for bicycle racing. Even the most garish of team kit is often wholly obliterated by mud. It became known as the 'Hell of the North', though not for its annual display of mud, dust and calamity, but for the devastated route as it appeared after World War I.

Given the nature of the race, with its 28 sections of cobbles, a large and growing part of the professional peloton choose not to enter it, despite the attraction of World Championships points, judging the risk of serious injury too high and the chances of avoiding random misfortune too low.

Koppenberg

Evocatively named after the Dutch term for cobbles –
kinderkoppen, children's heads – the Koppenberg is a notorious
obstacle that since 1976 has featured on the Tour of Flanders,
regularly causing carnage. A short but brutally steep climb
(only 77m, or 250ft) surfaced with the lethal Flandrien *pavés*,
it is hard to ride when dry and offers almost no traction when
wet: its gradient means that once you stop, or fall, or are
impeded by the fallen, or are simply blocked by the mass of the
race as it chokes the narrow lane, it is impossible to remount.
A lot of bikes are carried up the Koppenberg. In 1987, while
leading the race, Jesper Skibby was mown down by the race
commissaire's car as it tried to pass him on the climb. It was
15 years before a widened and improved Koppenberg was once
again included on the Tour of Flanders.

Liège–Bastogne–Liège is raced through quotidian, post-industrial suburbs.

Rather than sprinting, climbing or time-trialling ability, the ability to endure in the face of monumentally awful conditions could just be the quality that is most likely to triumph in Paris–Roubaix.

Yet in spite of the conditions some riders keep coming back for more: Roger De Vlaeminck and Tom Boonen have four wins apiece.

Liège–Bastogne–Liège
1892

A 250km (155mi) round trip through the pastoral Ardennes region of Belgium and back to the industrial suburbs of Liège. The oldest Classic, it has been run since 1892 and is respectfully known as 'La Doyenne'. Held to be the hardest of the five, it has a level outward leg that culminates in a series of severe climbs towards the finish, notably the Côte de Saint-Nicolas. While the Grand Tours aim to impress with a backdrop of Europe's most breath-taking natural and historic scenery, this Belgian Classic retains a solidly democratic landscape of dour north-ern industrial suburbs, climbing through some very ordinary streets. Run in April it is liable to extremes of weather: Bernard Hinault's 'Neige–Bastogne–Neige' victory in 1980 is famous for the snow (neige) that enveloped the race for its whole course, forcing the retirement of most of the field. Hinault, who wore a red woollen balaclava helmet and crust of snow for much of the race, took three weeks to regain the feeling in his hands. Eddy Merckx holds the record with five wins, one of them, in 1971, another snow-swept feat of endurance.

Trouée d'Arenberg

A gently sloping, arrow-straight cobbled road – pavé – 2.5km (1.5mi) long through a miserable forest in the post-industrial north of France has become the heart of Paris–Roubaix. It was added to the race in 1968 when roads this bad were becoming hard to find and it was feared that gentrification would tarmac the last of them. Pioneered by ex-miner and Vuelta winner Jean Stablinski, it is more likely to sabotage a rider's race than be the scene of his triumph. In the past it was possible to take the cinder path on either side of the cobbles, but now these are fenced off, and there is nowhere to ride but on the stones. The pavé is unpredictable under the best of conditions, and conditions are usually appalling, regularly seeming totally unviable for racing. Any prediction for the outcome is conditional on the very high possibility of random catastrophe caused by the cobbles. To make matters worse, the surface is further compromised by subsidence from mines beneath it and the removal of stones by fans.

The Tour de France took in some pavé in 2014, to the dismay of many teams. Predictably, poor weather resulted in notable casualties.

Giro di Lombardia
1905

In October comes the 'Classica delle Foglie Morte' (Classic of the Falling Leaves). The final Monument of the season, it marks the climax of a series of late-autumn Italian races. The 'Falling Leaves' is now a climber's race around Lake Como, having evolved since its inception in 1905 through various routes centred on Milan. It is a notably domestic affair, with more than half of its winners being Italian. Fausto Coppi holds the record with five wins, with Binda, Girardengo and Bartali among those with three each.

The Giro di Lombardia is notable for the Madonna del Ghisallo: on a hill close to Lake Como the Virgin Mary is said to have appeared to rescue the local medieval count from bandits. A shrine dedicated to the apparition was on the route of both the Giro di Lombardia and Giro d'Ita-lia, inspiring tifoso Pope Pius XII to recognize the Madonna del Ghisallo as the patron saint of cyclists in 1949. The shrine now houses relics such as bikes raced by Merckx, Moser and Coppi, signed maillots of Binda, Mario Cipollini and Gianni Bugno, and pennants, cycling ephemera and memorabilia of all types. Bicycles lean on the altar, and the one ridden by Fabio Casartelli when he died in the 1995 Tour de France is mounted on the wall.

Races, Rides and Climbs

Dumfries–Glasgow
1842

The first event that might, at a stretch, be called a bicycle race took place in 1842. Kirkpatrick Macmillan, a blacksmith from Dumfries, conceived and built himself a machine, powered by cranks and rods, and fitted with brakes. He used this to race the mail coach the 109km (68mi) from Dumfries to Glasgow. On arrival, after two days of riding, he was fined 5 shillings for 'furious driving', having collided with a child. Macmillan was the first person to devise a machine that offered a mechanical advantage, the first to fit brakes and, seemingly, the first to build something that could be ridden for sustained periods without contact with the ground. No detailed plan of his vehicle survives, though, and his innovations were forgotten.

Parc de Saint-Cloud
1868

The first formal race, now celebrated as being the beginning of cycling as a sport, took place in the Bois de Boulogne, Paris, on 31 May 1868. The 1,200m (3,937ft) dash through the Parc de Saint-Cloud was won by Englishman James Moore on a wooden Michaux Velocipede, with iron down- and top-tubes, and flattened iron wheels. The pedals were fixed directly to the axle, giving a 1:1 ratio. (This is also, however, the first disputed record in cycling, with many believing that there had already been a race earlier in the day, won by Edward Charles Bon. Or a mysterious other, named 'Polocini'.)

Moore went on to dominate the sport, winning both races arranged for that day, and the next milestone in cycling history – a road race between Paris and Rouen the following year. The bicycle he used for this is unknown, having been stolen from outside the victory celebrations. Moore later set an Hour Record of 23.3km (14.47mi) in the grounds of Molineux House in Wolverhampton.

One day after the Parc de Saint-Cloud event the first British race was held at the Welsh Harp reservoir, North London, and won by Arthur Markham.

Catford Hill Climb
1887

The oldest continuing bicycle race in the world, Catford Cycling Club's hill climb takes a short route up the North Downs, south of London. It was first run in 1887, with S.F. Edge winning on his innovative Safety bicycle, beating 11 other Safeties, tricycles and a single Ordinary up the seemingly impassable Westerham Hill. A minimum weight limit of 30kg (66lb) was enforced on all the single-speed machines.

Run over several local roads, the accepted home of the race is now Yorks Hill, a 646m (2,119ft) climb with a gradient reaching 25 per cent in places. The record time is 1'47.6", attained in 1983 by Phil Mason.

UCI Road World Championships
1927

This peripatetic race has been run in September or October since 1927. Organized around national rather than commercially sponsored teams, it is a single road race that decides the World Road Cycling Champion. The first winner was Binda, who – like Merckx, the Belgian Rik Van Steenbergen and Spaniard Óscar Freire – went on to win it three times. Nationally, Belgium has scored the most wins. The character of the course varies according to the venue, variously favouring sprinters, climbers, *puncheurs* or *randonneurs*. The course may be a circuit, a circular route or a one-way trip.

UCI World Tour

The World Tour is a season-long championship, culminating in a World Champion. It has mutated over time as cycling's governing bodies and the franchise holders of the Grand Tours have wrestled for power, influence and advertising revenue.

The current competition includes more than twenty events in the men's cycling season, with a system of points awarded, accumulating to decide the champion. There are also individual men's and women's, team, and national results at stake.

Yorks Hill persists as the venue for the longest continually run bicycle race in the world.

Racing Ordinaries in the Parc de Saint-Cloud.

Races on the World Tour include the three Grand Tours and Five Monuments, as well as a collection of other races of varying provenance. Most are in Europe, but Australia and Canada hold qualifying events, and the World Tour is extending into America and the Middle East, as young, exotic tours are included. The Tour de France will get you 200 UCI World Tour Championship points, while you'll get 80 for the Flèche Wallonne in Belgium.

Cycle racing at its highest level held out for a long time as an 'old world' concern, sticking resolutely to the roads of its origins: continental Western Europe. The UCI World Tour is, however, slowly starting to recognize the rest of the world, embracing races in Canada (since 2010), Australia (2008) and California (2017) as part of the Pro Tour.

Separate tours exist for Africa, Oceania, Europe, Asia and America, opening the prospect of a more global reach in professional cycling. An African wore a category jersey of the Tour de France for the first time in 2015, Daniel Teklehaimanot from Eritrea being King of the Mountains for three days.

Tour Down Under

Since 1999 this hugely popular week-long stage race has been held around Adelaide. For economic reasons the race has no time-trial stages (each rider can bring just one bike), and the landscape of South Australia offers little climbing, making this a race for the sprinters. Run in January, it is often punishingly hot.

Grand Prix Cycliste de Québec

Held in September in Québec City, Canada, this one-day race comprises 11 circuits of a hilly 18km (11.2mi) course.

Grand Prix Cycliste de Montréal

Two days after the Québec race, Montréal repeats the formula, with 17 laps of a 12km (7.45mi) circuit.

Tour of California

Incredibly, the United States spent the first hundred years of cycle-racing history isolated from world events. After Marshall Walter 'Major' Taylor went home, having successfully competed in Europe and Australasia until 1910, no American was noticed in Europe until Andy Hampsten won the snow-caked Giro in 1988. He was followed by Greg LeMond, with three Grand Tours and a Road World Championship. After that, Lance Armstrong's dominant personality overshadowed international cycling for a decade, only to have the whole period obliterated from the records when he eventually confessed to comprehensive doping throughout his regime. He was closely followed by Floyd Landis, who similarly impressed, albeit briefly, but was subsequently deleted for the same reasons.

The peloton now regularly features competitive Americans, and it is only fitting that the Tour of California should be included by the UCI, even if the long-term contribution made by South American riders might have argued in favour of the Vuelta de Colombia's getting in first.

The Tour of California, established in 2006, lasts eight days and takes in all the landscapes of the Golden State. Run in May, it competes with the Giro, but serves as a warm-up for the Tour de France.

'Triple Crown'

The 'Triple Crown' is the unofficial crowning achievement in cycling: two Grand Tours and the World Championship in the same year. Only achieved twice, by Eddy Merckx in 1974 and Stephen Roche in 1987, it is unlikely to happen again as riders increasingly concentrate their season on specific objectives, abandoning the possibility of multiple successes. In fact, only ten riders have ever won two Grand Tours in one year, and only eight have won a Grand Tour and the World Championship.

Tour of Britain

Between 1958 and 1993 the Milk Race was Britain's own stage race. It was sponsored by Britain's Milk Marketing Board (MMB), in what was a less commercially complicated world.

The race itself was born out of a controversial attempt to establish a mass-start, major stage race in the 1940s. At first a ramshackle affair, it was run on a shoestring budget, making its survival precarious until it was saved by milk. A primitive form of jersey sponsorship was suggested to the MMB, which instead decided to back a fully fledged tour. For 35 years the Milk Race was Britain's domestic Grand Tour, until the British milk market was deregulated and the MMB lost its crucial role.

After a brief period of sponsorship by breakfast cereal manufacturer Kellogg's, the event evolved into the more plainly titled Tour of Britain.

The Milk Race: Britain's premier road race for 35 years rewarded victory with a stuffed tiger.

Riders

A selection of personalities who have
shaped, defined and refined road racing.
Many, many more could be added...

Jacques Anquetil (FR)

Jacques Anquetil had eight Grand Tour victories (five Tours de France, two Giros and a Vuelta), and was indisputably the most handsome man to achieve podium places in any of these races. He was the most successful cyclist of his day, achieving 200 road race victories in his career. The first to win all three Grand Tours, he was, though, never a popular figure, openly declaring money to be his main motivation, and displaying a cold, mechanical personality and approach to racing. His regulated approach to competing earned him the nickname 'Monsieur Chrono' (chronometer). He built his success on unassailable time-trial performances, and it was his rival, the eternally second-placed Raymond Poulidor, who won the public's affection. The shoulder-to-shoulder battle of Poulidor and Anquetil on the Puy de Dôme in 1964 is one of cycling's most evocative images. Poulidor, the better climber, took the stage, but Anquetil had done enough to ensure that his advantage in the next day's time trial would secure his overall Tour victory. Anquetil also had a reputation as a gourmand and bon viveur, sometimes underperforming as a result of overindulgence.

Lance Armstrong (USA)

Lance Armstrong was the overwhelming force in racing at the start of the twenty-first century. His career spanned a promising start, acute illness followed by miraculous recovery, total domination of his sport, and then, ultimately, a complete negation of all his results and total disgrace. Armstrong went from being the poster boy for elite sport to the icon of everything that went wrong with racing and the crisis of doping.

He was always under suspicion, but the more he was accused, the harder he denied it. Journalists and governing bodies pursued him, but were met by an aggressive denial at every stage. Eventually, cracks appeared in the mountain of Armstrong's myth, and his drug-saturated regime was exposed as teammates, journalists and pharmacists all began to talk. His seven wins in the Tour de France

were all declared void, and he seemed set to appear only in court from there on. Armstrong chose to confess to his doping on *The Oprah Winfrey Show*, broadcast across two successive nights on prime-time TV in 2013. His performance in that interview has been meticulously scrutinized for any traces of sincerity or contrition. His seven victories in the Tour de France have been left blank in the records.

Alfredo Binda (IT)

Alfredo Binda was the man who was paid to stay away from the race – the Giro of 1930 – to give others a chance. Binda won more Giros than any other rider (five), beginning in 1927 and securing his last in 1933. It was 2004 before Mario Cipollini eventually achieved more stage victories in the race than Binda. His rationality and perceived coldness, though, meant that for all his success, he failed to win the affection of the public and made himself even less popular by deposing Costante Girardengo, the revered incumbent hero of Italian cycling. Popular allegiance instead went first to Domenico Piemontesi and then to Learco Guerra, Girardengo's anointed successor. But Binda was unstoppable, and with five Giros and three World Championships, eventually the *tifosi* had to concede their respect, if not affection. Rather more modestly, Binda's name endured longest on his brand of toe straps.

Chris Boardman (UK)

Three times World Hour Record holder, three days yellow jersey wearer, and three times prologue stage winner of the Tour de France, Chris Boardman led the advance of British cycling in the 1990s. A time-trial specialist, Boardman's first Tour de France stage was, at the time, the race's fastest ever win. The following year, though, he crashed spectacularly in the rain and was then hit by his team car. Boardman's track riding became his most successful phase, increasing the World Hour Record three times in a succession of duels with Graeme Obree, Miguel Induráin, Francesco Moser and Tony Rominger.

Ottavio Bottecchia (IT)

Born in 1894, the poverty of his origins seemed to remain with Ottavio Bottecchia even after his triumphs. The first Italian winner of the Tour de France, in 1924, he had spent World War I smuggling messages and supplies across the mountains on a folding bike. Turning professional in 1920, he finished fifth in the 1923 Giro, attracting the attention of the AuToMoTo team, which enlisted him for the Tour de France. He arrived in France threadbare and weatherbeaten, speaking barely any French, but won a stage and placed second overall. As predicted, the following year he won the Tour, leading the race for its duration. He won again in 1925, aided by Lucien Buysse, the first domestique to help secure a win. That, though, was the end of his success. He abandoned the 1926 Tour in tears, fleeing an apocalyptic deluge. His form disappeared as he retreated to Italy demoralized and nervous of his health. In June 1927 his body was found on a country road, next to his undamaged bicycle. One month previously his brother had died in similar circumstances. The events surrounding his death have never been ascertained, though several theories have been suggested: an accident, assassination by Fascists for his socialist leanings, or felled by a rock thrown by a farmer who caught him stealing grapes.

Mark Cavendish (UK)

The epitome of British cycling's successes in the early 2000s, in numbers Mark Cavendish is the most successful British cyclist ever. The 'Manx Missile' has only Merckx ahead of him in Tour de France stage wins (30 to 34), four achieved consecutively on the Champs-Élysées. He has won the points jerseys of all three Grand Tours, and worn both the *maglia rosa* and the *maillot jaune*. A current total of 48 Grand Tour victories places him all-time third, behind Mario Cipollini (64) and Merckx (57). He is also a World Road Cycling Champion, World Champion in the Madison (a team track event), Olympic medallist, and winner of Milan–San Remo. In 2014, though, his home crowd was disappointed to see him end his Tour de France on the tarmac in Harrogate, Yorkshire, at the end of Stage 1.

Cavendish is a sprinter, all his road victories coming from out of the bunch in the last few metres. The way he has imposed himself in some finishes has attracted official penalties on occasions, and generated some ill-feeling in the peloton. This could, however, be seen as an unavoidable consequence of his craft. As well as huge power and spectacular acceleration, Cavendish possesses an extraordinary memory for course conditions, being able to recall the final metres of race stages in minute detail.

Mario Cipollini (IT)

Mario Cipollini was the most dandified, exhibitionist cyclist of his time. Costume sometimes seemed as important to him as performance, and he collected fines for selecting racewear of his own preference rather than what was defined in the rules of the race, once even appearing as a Roman senator. His wardrobe and grooming, together with presumptions about his conduct off the bike,

threatened to eclipse his achievements on it. Yet for all his flamboyance, and surrounding frenzy, 'Super Mario' was a hugely impressive athlete, advancing the discipline of sprinting as the first rider to deploy a sprint train to deliver him to the front. He won more stages of the Giro than any other rider, his 42 finally ending Binda's ownership of the race, and sprinted to 12 stage wins in the Tour de France, four on

consecutive days in 1999. Cipollini was a specialist: while he made a point of finishing the Giro, on the Tour he did all his work in the first week and then went home, reluctant to drag all that heavy muscle over the mountains.

His testosterone level was said to have been raised by pictures of Pamela Anderson taped to his frame, though he was also implicated in heavy doping programmes.

Fausto Coppi (IT)

Fausto Coppi dominated cycling either side of World War II, untouchable by anyone. Without the enforced lay-off due to hostilities, when Coppi was in his early twenties and would have been at his strongest, it seems certain that he would have bettered the record of Merckx to be the most successful rider ever. When he rode away from the peloton, he was never caught. His margins were regularly over ten minutes on the field. Prize money for the lower placings was increased just to encourage the also-rans to continue under his relentless domination. The first man to win the Giro and the Tour in the same year, which he did twice, he racked up five Giros, two Tours, the Hour Record, Paris–Roubaix, Milan–San Remo, the Flèche Wallonne – everything. Coppi could climb, sprint and time trial.

The spur to Coppi's performance was his rivalry with Gino Bartali, Italy's 'Other Cyclist'. Bartali was the Southern traditionalist, while Coppi was the modern man from the North. Coppi had been taken on as Bartali's domestique for the 1940 Giro, but instead took the race. From then on, theirs was an intense personal rivalry: it engulfed their tactics and performance and verged on childlike in their commitment to it. At the 1948 World Championships they both effectively retired as each waited for the other to make his move while the rest of the field carried on the race.

The definitive performance of Coppi's career was probably in the 1949 Giro. On a 254km (158mi) stage, with five Category 1 climbs, he attacked on the first and rode the rest alone, finishing over 11 minutes ahead of the next rider, Bartali.

Coppi's descent from favour, however, was nearly as dramatic as his rise. In the mid-1950s he left his wife to begin an affair with 'La Dama Bianca', the mysterious woman in white who had been seen greeting him

a bit too enthusiastically on the finish line. Catholic Italy was scandalized, and the public turned violently against him. Even the Pope urged him to reconcile with his wife, but he left her to live with Giulia Ochini, while his form collapsed and he struggled even to finish races. In 1959 he was invited to take part in an exhibition race and a safari by the president of Burkina Faso. There he fell victim to virulent mosquitoes, and died on his return to Italy. Inevitably, there followed rumours of conspiracy and foul play.

Coppi is believed to have doped frequently, taking a more modern, methodical approach to chemical assistance, which at the time was not banned: Bartali would even examine Coppi's trash to learn what to expect in the day's racing. Bartali declared, you can only assume grudgingly, that 'On a bike, Fausto was like a god. When we got off he was a mortal, but when he pedalled he was supernatural.'

He is memorialized at the Giro every year, where the winner of the highest mountain stage is awarded the 'Cima Coppi'.

Aluminium Cannondale CAAD 3 Time Trial bike, 1999, weapon of choice for Mario Cipollini.

Roger De Vlaeminck (BE)

Belgian Roger De Vlaeminck never won a Grand Tour, but was the most successful rider in the Monuments ever. Emerging from cyclocross in the early 1970s, De Vlaeminck went on to win Paris–Roubaix a record four times – as well as every other Monument. Only Merckx was more successful than De Vlaeminck in the great one-day races, and it is possible that he would have won more had team politics not compromised his competitiveness for several years. Four times winner of the points jersey in the Giro, he was never a finisher in the Tour de France. He epitomizes the hard-man image of Northern European cycling and now regularly likes to complain that cycling is not as hard as it was when he was racing.

Henri Desgrange (FR)

The first person to set a recognized Hour Record for cycling, Henri Desgrange was a competitor, but better remembered as the newspaper man who conceived and realized the Tour de France in 1903, inventing the bicycle stage race and incidentally introducing the French to the shape of their own country. Desgrange owned the Tour, and it was run by his rules, from setting the route, to the specification of the bikes, to when riders might be allowed to remove items of clothing. Infringements were dealt with severely. A fanatical believer in the moral improvement that rigorous sport would bring to his country, Desgrange's ideal race would have only one finisher, the rest of the field tested beyond endurance. His dictatorial regime was legendary: in 1934, after André Leducq defected from the Alcyon team to Mercier, and was dropped from the French team at the request of the indignant Alcyon director, Desgrange commanded his newspaper to persistently misspell the name of Mercier, eventually settling on 'Merdier'. Desgrange continues to be celebrated on the Tour by his monogram on the yellow jersey.

Hélène Dutrieu (BE/FR)

At a point when the bicycle was still an exotic innovation, Belgian-born Hélène Dutrieu straddled the gap between sport and circus. She achieved the women's Hour Record in 1893, and made appearances demonstrating her daring execution as 'La Flèche Humaine' (The Human Arrow), jumping a 15m (49ft) span. She broke the 40km (25mi) barrier in the women's (Paced) Hour Record, and was twice World Track Champion. She was part of the elite squad assembled by William Spears Simpson that campaigned in Britain to promote his Lever Chain mechanism.

Along with fellow female cyclist Marie Marvingt (La Fiancée du Danger), La Flèche Humaine moved from cycling into aviation and became known for her couture flying suits. Never lacking courage, she then drove ambulances in World War I.

Chris Froome (UK)

Riding first for Kenya, then joining the Sky team as a Briton, Chris Froome was first a domestique supporting Bradley Wiggins's 2012 Tour de France win before becoming record-breaking in his own right. His first big success had come in 2011, when he finished second in the Vuelta to equal the best ever Grand Tour placing for a British rider. Released from domestique service, he won his first Tour de France in 2013, did not finish in 2014, then won the following two years. In 2017, when it was starting to seem that no one would ever win more than one Grand Tour in a season again, Froome took the Tour de France and the Vuelta a España, becoming one of only ten riders to achieve such multiple victories in the same year. He has won the Critérium du Dauphiné three times, the Tour of Romandie twice and the Tour of Oman twice.

Riding in the post-Armstrong atmosphere of suspicion and distrust, Froome's sudden appearance on podiums attracted severe scrutiny and persistent accusations of doping and even of motorized assistance. Constant demands have been made for minutely detailed records of his physiological statistics. Laboratory testing suggests that he is viable and not 'mutant', as his performance has been euphemistically described. Despite this he continues to attract roadside accusations, culminating in a dousing with a spectator's urine in 2015.

For all his success, the enduring image of Froome might become the one of him without his bike, running up Mont Ventoux in a chaotic melee of fans and support cars, after a shunt with a motorbike on his way to winning the 2016 Tour de France.

Maurice Garin (FR)

Known as 'The Little Sweep' because of his childhood occupation, Maurice Garin was the winner of the first Tour de France in 1903. Garin rode the almost 2,500km (1,550mi) circuit of France in six days, later writing to Desgrange that he had felt like a bull pierced by banderillas as he rode. He won the second Tour, but was disqualified for cheating, in a race marked by violence and disorder. After shots were fired to clear the crowds, and Garin and eight other riders had been disqualified, the race was awarded to nineteen-year-old Henri Cornet, who had finished fourth on tyres flattened by nails. Records detailing the exact nature of Garin's offences were lost when the Tour archive was moved to escape the Nazis, but years later a man remembered Garin telling him that he had used a train to cover part of the course.

Costante Girardengo (IT)

Costante Girardengo was the great Italian cyclist of the early 1900s, and the first rider to be declared *campionissimo* (champion of champions). 'The Novi Runt' won the Giro twice, where his 30 stage wins still keep him in the top five of all time. He also won Milan–San Remo, the Giro di Lombardia and nine Italian Road Race Championships.

Immensely popular with the public, he would possibly have won more, but for the interruption of World War I, and the notorious temperament that led him to several unwise retirements. He is memorialized in Italy in the popular song 'Il Bandito e il Campione' (The Bandit and the Champion), which records his friendship with a notorious local gangster.

Bernard Hinault (FR)

Bernard Hinault was known as 'Le Blaireau' (The Badger) – not particularly glamorous, but he was the undisputed ruler of the peloton throughout the 1980s. One of the best-known images of the dictatorial and pugnacious Hinault shows him brawling with striking workers blocking the route on the Paris–Nice race in 1984. He is the closest to Merckx in his *palmarès*: ten Grand Tours, and the only rider to win each at least twice, multiple Monuments,

stage races and time trials. His domination was absolute.

The most controversial of his races, though, were his two final Tours de France: his last victory in 1985 and the following year when he came second to Greg LeMond. In 1985 Hinault was to be supported by the rising talent LeMond, the big-budget American signing to the very French La Vie Claire team. Hinault won the race, but the relationship between the two was

tense. The accepted story was that Hinault promised the 1986 race to LeMond if he would support him to win in 1985. LeMond felt tethered by team discipline, and discriminated against due to his lack of Frenchness in 1985, but the race went the way Hinault directed. The following year, though, Hinault's promised support of LeMond was delivered ambiguously; nevertheless, the young American succeeded in deposing the old French badger.

Miguel Induráin (ES)

Miguel Induráin is the only five-time consecutive winner of the Tour de France (1991–95), one of seven to win a Tour and a Giro in the same year, Olympic Champion in 1996 and World Time Trial Champion in 1995. Of his 14 stage wins in the Grand Tours, only two were not for time trials. Unbeatable against the clock, he would limit his losses in the mountains and won races more by attrition than by attacks. His power was unstoppable, but he did not provide the spectacle of other champions: tactically faultless rather than inspired.

Induráin was declared a physiological phenomenon: heartrate, lung capacity, oxygen consumption and blood flow were all at almost superhuman levels. This did not stop suspicions that such overwhelming power could not have been produced without chemical assistance. He has, however, never tested positive for any banned substances.

Théodore Joyeux (FR)

While Henri Desgrange is the accepted architect and czar of the Tour de France, the real origin of what was to become the best race in the world lay in the rivalry between a barber from Lot-et-Garonne and an engineer from Brittany. At a time when epic endeavours of pioneering sportsmen gripped the public imagination, Théodore Joyeux and Jean-Marie Corre both proposed a *tour de France*, making the hitherto unthinkable circuit by bicycle. It was Joyeux on a shaft-driven Métropole Acatène who got round first, taking 19 days to cover the 5,500km (3,415mi) in May 1895. Corre then followed him round in September.

Greg LeMond (USA)

The first American to breach the European Classics, Greg LeMond won out in two of the Tour de France's most dramatic races, ending Hinault's reign in 1986 and beating Laurent Fignon by just eight seconds to win the 1989 race. He was the first American to be the World Road Racing Champion. A skier who turned to cycling for off-season training, LeMond entered the European peloton in 1981 and was immediately a contender for the big races. Initially frustrated at having to ride as a domestique, he placed third in his first Tour de France supporting Fignon, and second in the next riding for Hinault. It was understood that the following year Hinault would repay the service, but the Frenchman appeared to attack LeMond and at times left him isolated. They smiled and shook hands at the top of the Alpe d'Huez, where they finished together, LeMond in yellow with Hinault taking the stage, but the agreement was barely evident throughout the rest of the race. LeMond won by three minutes, the first, and the only American to win a Grand Tour now that both Floyd Landis and Lance Armstrong have been disqualified.

In 1987, LeMond was seriously injured in a hunting accident, and it was 1989 before he raced again. Bringing with him innovative aero bars and helmet, and a carbon bike, he beat Laurent Fignon in the final time trial on the Champs-Élysées by eight seconds, after 3,285km (2,041mi) of racing, the narrowest margin ever. LeMond successfully defended his title in 1990, but from then on he struggled to find his best form. He retired in 1994, suspicion falling on the 35 pellets of lead shot left in his body after the accident for having caused poisoning that left him uncompetitive.

LeMond was, and remains, a strident voice against doping in the sport, a stance which earned him the wrath of Lance Armstrong, whose sponsor Trek abandoned LeMond's line of racing bikes in retribution for his criticism of their star at his zenith.

Marie Marvingt (FR)

Marie Marvingt, La Fiancée du Danger, was born in France in 1875 and vigorously defied the restrictions on her gender by engaging in apparently every sport going. She attempted to enter the 1908 Tour de France, believing herself qualified after having ridden 1,400km (870mi) to view the eruption of a volcano in Italy. She was excluded, but rode the whole route behind the race to the finish in Paris. Her time was unrecorded, but she performed better than the two-thirds of the all-male peloton that retired. This cycling milestone was just a sideline in her prodigious list of achievements, which included fighting in World War I disguised as a man, inventing the air ambulance and ballooning across the North Sea. Heavily decorated by the French state, she remains the unique recipient of a Médaille d'Or from the Académie des Sports, fittingly 'for all sports'.

Eddy Merckx (BE)

Édouard Merckx was born in 1945, the son of a Belgian grocer. In 1996 he was elevated to Baron, unarguably the most successful racing cyclist of all time. He never won the Paris–Tours Classic, but he did win everything else.

Amateur World Champion at 19, Merckx turned professional in 1965 and won his first Classic, Milan–San Remo, in 1966. He won it again the following year, and in 1969, 1971, 1975 and 1976. In total he took 525 professional races. Merckx won every other Classic, the three Grand Tours,

the World Championship and held the World Hour Record for twelve years.

The 1969 Tour de France marked the most comprehensive domination of the race ever: he held the yellow, green, white and polka-dot jerseys, along with team and combativity awards. Stage 17, Luchon to Mourenx, was his greatest ever performance: he rode 140km (87mi) alone, over five cols, to finish eight minutes before the next rider. He was already in yellow, with more than eight minutes in hand, and could easily have controlled the race from within the peloton.

'The Cannibal' consumed anyone who threatened his professional reign, from 1968 to 1975. But not everyone loved him for it. Like Binda, who won the Giro too often, and Coppi, who wore out the affection of his fans, Merckx's comprehensive domination alienated a public that thirsted for drama and relished the unpredictable. Merckx only offered inevitability. He was resented particularly in France, for his annexation of the Tour, and his absence in 1974 was rumoured to have been at the request of the organizers.

But of course he was eventually vulnerable. At the end of 1969, a crash in a derny race (that is, paced behind a motorbike, or derny) left his pacer dead and Merckx with a cracked vertebra and twisted pelvis. He said he was never the same rider again. Constant pain drove him to endless adjustments to his bike in search of some relief. The spectacle that had denied the fans at his peak began as his dominance faltered. In the 1971 Tour Luis Ocaña proved that time could be taken from the Cannibal, and Merckx only escaped the threat when a deluge over the Pyrenees washed Ocaña out of the race.

After that, though he was to go on winning Grand Tours until 1974, it was the spectacle of the peloton reeling in the Cannibal that fed the crowds, and it was Thévenet – a Frenchman – who bested him in the 1975 Tour. Merckx fought Bernard Thévenet (and the whole of France) as he strived to better Anquetil's record five Tour victories. On Stage 14, leading the race, he was punched in the back by a drunk fan. He recovered sufficiently to maintain his lead, but lost it to Thévenet the next day. On Stage 17 Merckx crashed, breaking his jaw. He continued, contending to the end, and finished the race in second place, but by then it was clear that the Cannibal had himself been consumed.

James Moore (UK)

James Moore, from Suffolk, England, believed himself to be the winner of the first formal bicycle race. On 31 May 1868 he rode his iron-tyred wooden-framed Michaux Velocipede to win a 1,200m (3,940ft) race in the Parc de Saint-Cloud in the Bois de Boulogne in Paris. Moore went on to dominate the sport, winning both of the races arranged for that day, as well as the next milestone in cycling history, a road race between Paris and Rouen later the same year.

Luis Ocaña (ES)

Luis Ocaña was the Spanish National Champion and winner of the 1970 Vuelta and 1973 Tour. The dramatic apex of his career was 1971, the year he believed he could depose Merckx. After 13 stages in the Tour Ocaña had built an eight-minute lead. On Stage 14, Revel to Luchon, Merckx rode furiously and attacked in the mountains but he could do nothing to claw back the time. At the top of the Col de Menté, in the Pyrenees, a deluge enveloped the race. Already wrapped in fog and battered by torrential rain

and hail storms, the roads became running streams. Merckx, Ocaña, Joop Zoetemelk and Lucien Van Impe plunged down the mountain together, Merckx desperate to escape and Ocaña determined to stay with him. Halfway down Merckx failed to take a corner and crashed. Ocaña followed him, crashing over a low wall. Zoetemelk and Van Impe followed. Merckx remounted and continued his descent along with the other two, but Ocaña was left on the ground, cradled by spectators, until he was lifted from

the mountain in a helicopter, while Merckx went on to take the Tour.

The following year Ocaña retired from the Tour with bronchitis, so it was 1973 before he won the race, but it was a race without Merckx. He never beat the Cannibal.

The crash on the Col de Menté was the epitome of a whole catalogue of incidents that earned Ocaña the reputation as the unluckiest man in cycling. Ocaña shot himself in 1977, in poor health and having been disappointed in business.

Marco Pantani (IT)

At 1.7m (5ft 7in) and 57kg (126lb), Marco Pantani was a pure climber. The last rider to win the Tour de France and the Giro in the same year (1998), he was inspired but erratic, replacing the mechanistic domination of Miguel Induráin with performances of unpredictable brilliance that alternated with periods of disillusion. In 1998, after winning the Giro, he devastated Jan Ullrich's early lead in the Tour. On Stage 15, Grenoble to Les Deux Alpes, over the Croix de Fer, Galibier and Les Deux Alpes, he took nine minutes from Ullrich to lead the race, which he won by 3'21".

Pantani claimed that the fear induced by the 'Festina Affair' drug raids had left the 1998 Tour the cleanest ever. The following year, though, while leading the Giro, an unannounced blood test before the start at Madonna di Campiglio found his blood to be too rich, at 52 per cent hematocrit, and he was thrown off the race. This seemed to be the beginning of the unravelling of Pantani, as he struggled to regain his credibility and form. In the 2000 Tour he matched Lance Armstrong on Mont Ventoux, but this was the last flourish before his genius became ever more elusive, and despite some great stage performances he never won another big race. Drugs – recreational rather than performance enhancing – took over his life, as he struggled against perceived conspiracy and victimization. He died in 2004, from cocaine poisoning.

Stephen Roche (IR)

Stepehen Roche's year was 1987. In May he won the Giro, earning the enduring wrath of Itay's *tifosi* on the way when he defied team orders and took the *maglia rosa* when he should have been supporting his teammate. Roche rode the rest of the race with police protection but no team support after this transgression, and the fury over Roche's individual success put against the conventions of team discipline contrived one of the most bitterly debated results of any Grand Tour. It did not help that it resulted in the absence of any Italians on the podium that year. In July Roche took his pariah status with him to the Tour de France, where his Carrera team continued his excommunication. Enlisting support from elsewhere, he took the race, crucially with a historic effort on La Plagne, where he chased down challenger Pedro Delgado, then collapsed at the mountain-top finish. The season ended with Roche winning the World Championships in Austria, joining Merckx as one of only two riders to have achieved a Triple Crown.

Alfonsina Strada (IT)

Alfonsina Strada is the only woman ever to have officially competed in a Grand Tour, the Giro d'Italia of 1924. At the time, no rule explicitly stated that women could not race against men, probably because no one could imagine it happening. Strada was a passionately competitive cyclist, racing on the bike she had demanded as her 'dowry' when she married. The Giro was depleted after World War I, and the organizers struggled to entice a viable field to enter. Strada had ensured her start by dropping the last 'a' from her first name on her entry form, and even when she appeared at the start organizers allowed her to race, probably deciding that the unimaginable spectacle of a woman competing would be good PR. She finished the race, persisting through the Giro's notorious extremes of weather, even riding one stage with a broom handle replacing her broken handlebars. She managed to overturn public outrage and received tributes, special prizes, new jerseys and earrings from the public, and even from Mussolini. She was, however, officially eliminated for being outside the time limit.

Strada went on to ride in exhibition races all over Europe, eventually settling down to run a bike shop in Milan. In 1959 she died of a heart attack trying to right her fallen motorcycle.

Marshall Walter 'Major' Taylor (USA)

Born in Indianapolis in the aftermath of the American Civil War, Marshall Walter Taylor was the world's best track cyclist of the 1890s. A clean-living devout Christian, he would not compete on Sundays, but won races and world records at all distances, from quarter-mile (400m) sprints to the then popular six-day events.

Having been given a bike by his father's rich white employers, Taylor immediately displayed prodigious talent as a cyclist. While working for a local bike shop, he started to race, decisively winning amateur events. Never in the army, Taylor dressed up in military costume to race, earning him his rank.

In Indianapolis, Taylor was met with intense racism. He was forced off the track, boxed in and had water thrown over him and nails thrown in front of his bike. He was even forced off his bike and strangled by a fellow athlete. Massachusetts bicycle manufacturer Louis D. 'Birdie' Munger saw Taylor's potential and took him to the more tolerant East Coast state, where his professional career began. Mentored by Munger, and supported by President Theodore Roosevelt, 'Major' Taylor quickly became America's fastest cyclist. Throughout his career, though, he was subjected to extreme racism, banned from racing in the Southern States, and impeded, assaulted and abused by other riders and crowds. Segregation was enforced by sporting institutions, and Taylor and Munger regularly received death threats. At one point, a desperate Munger was said to have tried to bleach Taylor's skin. Despite all this, 'Major' Taylor was an unstoppable force on the track, becoming World Champion in 1899, and American Sprint Champion in 1900, and setting world records at various distances.

In 1901 he was invited to race in France, where 'Le Nègre Volant'

(The Black Cyclone), was greeted as a cycling Messiah. Relieved after the hostility he attracted at home, he went on to tour Europe and Australasia.

In all, Taylor rode professionally for 14 years, and retired at 27, feeling that he was approaching his decline and exhausted by the persistent racism that met his successes. An unsuccessful return to racing followed, but his life declined dramatically away from the track, and he died destitute in Chicago in 1932.

Bradley Wiggins (UK)

Bradley Wiggins, son of an Australian professional cyclist, born on the Belgian cycling circuit, is the culmination of Britain's phenomenal cycling success at the beginning of the twenty-first century. Both Track and Time Trial World Champion, Olympic gold medallist, winner of Grand Tour and Classic stage races, Wiggins also broke the World Hour Record in 2015 and has won more than any other British cyclist.

Born in Ghent but raised in North London, Wiggins moved through track racing to road, achieving the international success that had eluded British cycling for years and ultimately becoming the first Briton to win the Tour de France. Wiggins went professional in 2001 with the short-lived Linda McCartney team, and while training with the British national squad his potential on the track began to show, after which he was mentored by Chris Boardman.

Having enjoyed considerable success on the track, including gold for the Individual Pursuit at the 2004 Athens Olympics, in 2007 he made his first mark on the Tour de France, receiving the combativity award for effort. Unfortunately, things went downhill from there, his whole team having to withdraw from the race after a positive drug test on another rider. Wiggins made clear his hardline stance on drugs, putting his Cofidis team kit in the bin on the way home.

At this time, he began his occasional partnership with Mark Cavendish, winning silver in the Madison team track event at the Beijing Olympics in 2008. As an individual, he won gold in Beijing, and also at the World Championships that same year.

By 2009 he was in contention for podium places in stage races as well, taking fourth place in the Tour, later upgraded to third when Lance Armstrong's doping violations moved everyone up a place. This made Wiggins the first Briton to achieve a podium placing in the Tour, even if technically he had not stood on it.

As a member of the black-clad Sky Team, his *annus mirabilis* was 2012, beginning with victories in Paris–Nice and the Tour de Romandie, and the successful defence of his Critérium du Dauphiné title. Wiggins started well in the Tour de France, taking the yellow jersey on Stage 7, to join the group of nine Britons who had worn it previously. Supported by Chris Froome, he kept the *maillot* all the way to Paris, winning both time-trial stages on the way. It had taken 108 years for a Briton to win the Tour, after Charles Holland rode it first in 1904.

In 2013 Wiggins declared an ambitious Giro/Tour double as his goal, but illness, injury and accident forced him to retire from both. Instead, he took the Tour of Britain. In a popular late-career move, he took the World Hour Record in 2015, raising it by nearly 1,600m (5,249ft). After another Olympic gold medal in Brazil in 2016 (in the team pursuit event), Wiggins finally retired.

A.A. *Zimmerman* (USA)

Arthur Augustus Zimmerman was an American sprint phenomenon from New Jersey whose performances in the 1890s dominated his sport in the United States and Britain and helped establish a World Championship. 'Zimmy' began racing at the age of 17, riding a Penny Farthing. In 1891 he reversed the configuration to race on a bicycle with the smaller wheel at the front, and on this he won the League of American Wheelman's Half-mile Championship with a world-record performance.

Zimmerman was known for pedalling at an exceptionally high cadence, earning him the nickname 'The Jersey Skeeter'. Argument persists, but rates of up to 160rpm have been claimed. Riding as an amateur all across the US, Zimmerman won horses, land, jewellery, bicycles and pianos, though on turning professional he requested payment in gold. He was American Champion in 1890, 1891 and 1892, and British Champion at 1 and 5 miles (1.6km and 8km) in 1892. In 1893 he won the first World Championships, both the sprint and the 10km (6mi).

As a professional he was sponsored by Raleigh and toured France, Britain and Australia as a celebrity sportsman, attracting huge crowds. Initially unimpressive – 'he looks as though he eats nothing but string' – he went on to embarrass local athletes to the point that he was asked to make races 'more interesting'. He responded by loitering at the back of the field until it seemed impossible to recover, then launching a sprint at breathtaking cadence to win at the very last minute. Zimmerman seems to have declined rapidly, and he failed to perform well in his last tours to Europe. After nine years of racing he retired to run a hotel in New Jersey.

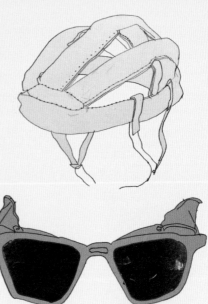

Kit

From woollen jerseys and long trousers worn with flying helmets and goggles to lycra skinsuits and pointy helmets: a century of iconic jerseys, technical innovations – and tight clothes.

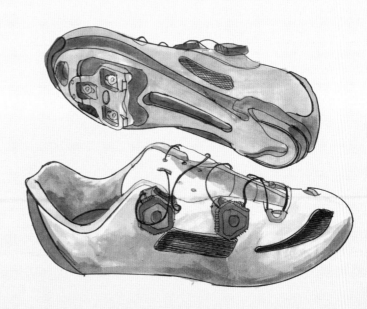

Maillots

Early racing was conducted in tweeds and wool, with flying helmets and goggles. There was little difference in costume between cyclists and early aviators. In 1910 Alfredo Binda had himself dressed by the tailor Vittore Gianni, inventing dedicated cycling kit.

Jerseys were long sleeved, with buttons across the shoulder and a pocket on the chest. In the 1940s, Fausto Coppi's personal tailor, Armando Castelli, introduced silk. As well as considerations of comfort and practicality, silk was better able to accept being printed with ink, which would become increasingly important as advertising increased.

Synthetics began to challenge wool in the late 1940s but were resisted by many. In 1947 Louis 'Louison' Bobet handed back his yellow jersey, rejecting its synthetic fibres – an awkward moment for the race organizers, since the jersey was actually sponsored by Sofil, the makers of the acrylic yarn.

Wool persisted right through the 1960s. The idea of climbing alpine stages wearing wool in August gives some idea of just how much suffering professional bike riders can endure.

Towards the end of the 1960s, the broad chest pocket, which never appeared to contain anything anyway, finally vanished, leaving the familiar three rear pockets as the standard.

In 1977 Maurizio Castelli, Armando's son, pioneered what was probably the most noticeable innovation to the sport since the pneumatic tyre: a woven polyurethane-polyurea copolymer fabric, marketed as 'lycra'. Again, performance went hand in hand with promotion as he developed a special dye process to better accept branding. In 1981 he broke the ban on anything but black shorts and in 1996 he debuted the skinsuit.

The last piece of natural fabric was dropped from the peloton in 1977 when the chamois leather pad was removed from the shorts to be replaced by 'technical' materials.

Cycling often takes on the appearance of an uncontrolled binge of branding. As teams replaced the individual, the logos of bicycle manufacturers started to appear on their chests: Hyalite, Elvish, Alcyon, Hutchinson, AuToMoTo. The logo at this point, though, was strictly relevant to the event.

In 1954 Nivea paid Fiorenzo Magni to wear a shirt branded with their logo – an unlikely association, Fiorenzo not being a conventional model for beauty products. (There was, however, a compelling connection between the product and the sport: it was used to soften the chamois leather in the shorts.) The link, nevertheless, between the sport and what was written across the chest (back, shoulders, thighs,

ankles and head) had been broken, and a spectacle of attention-stealing graphic exhibitionism was unleashed as the kit became an all-over branded suit, with matching *maillots*, mitts, caps, capes and bootees.

The fierce competition for prominence on the backs of riders has led to some remarkable kit, bringing a psychedelic quality to the peloton and fully exploiting the most vivid and fluorescent spectrums of print technology.

Team Mapei – sponsored by an Italian grout and tile-adhesive maker – impressed through the 1990s in remarkable harlequin-like geometry, while the jeans manufacturer Carrera's literal stance, with a faux denim kit, was possibly a low point in branding.

Now multiple sponsors fight for space on one shirt in a vivid confusion of branding. Niche marketing can even put a logo into an armpit.

Teams have been serially rebranded as the burden of financing them is passed on: Peugeot, for instance, become Z, which in turn became Crédit Agricole. In most cases, while instantly recognizable to fans, the activity of the sponsor is entirely forgotten. Banks, supermarkets, ice cream, pens, cable TV stations, builders' merchants and sausage suppliers can all leave a mark, but in many cases, while the name is remembered, what they actually did is never known.

AuToMoTo: A French maker of bicycles, motorbikes and cars, at a time when they were all made under the same roof. It was swallowed up by Peugeot, and gone by 1960.

Bartali: From 1948 until he retired in 1954, Gino Bartali rode bikes carrying his own name, made for him by the Santamaria brothers. Ursus is an Italian component manufacturer.

Bic: Maker of economy ballpoint pens and razors. The Baron Bich was a notoriously difficult customer and ended sponsorship in 1974 on bad terms.

Brooklyn: An Italian chewing gum with no connection to the New York borough at all – permanently stuck to the Belgian star Roger De Vlaeminck.

C&A: A Belgian team financed by the Dutch fashion giant in the late 1970s. It was a boldly logo-centric kit, the forerunner of Z's fluorescent pop *maillots*.

Carrera: The Italian jeans-maker had a high profile throughout the 1980s and 1990s, taking its work with denim very literally to produce some horrible kit.

Castorama: The French DIY store is another strong contender for the worst kit ever, with its bib and braces branding.

Faema: The Italian manufacturer of espresso machines produced perhaps Eddy Merckx's most iconic kit.

Ford: Ford's two-year association with cycling included a Tour de France win with Lucien Aimar in 1966.

La Vie Claire: The French health-food brand built a team around Bernard Hinault when he parted company with Renault. It had a bold Mondrian-inspired identity and was closely associated with LOOK.

Mapei: The Italian tile adhesives and grout maker produced one of the most graphically arresting kits of all time.

Molteni: The iconic kit of Eddy Merckx and possibly one of the least-recognizable brands. Molteni made Italian salami.

Nivea: The German face cream was the first *extrasportif* sponsor. Unkindly, reporters never failed to stress the irony of a beauty product advertised across the chest of the ruggedly unglamorous Fiorenzo Magni.

Peugeot: Bicycling was just one interest of the French industrial giant. One of the longest running brands in cycling, it was prominent in racing from its very beginnings until 1986.

Renault: The French car manufacturer ran a team from 1978 to 1985. It was the first home of Bernard Hinault before he was usurped by Laurent Fignon.

Sky: This black-clad force in the peloton of the 2010s represents the satellite arm of Rupert Murdoch's media colossus, a fittingly over-powering presence, provoking widely divided opinions.

Toshiba: Evolving out of the La Vie Claire team, Toshiba decided to continue the strong graphic identity of their kit. It often appears in lists of worst-dressed teams, though.

Vêtements Z: French children's clothing manufacturer, a pop art classic from the 1980s.

Eyewear

Early riders wore goggles, which were essential on unsealed roads to protect from dust and mud. They were often worn in combination with a cap or even a flying helmet, making riders look like pilots. In the 1950s, as road surfaces improved and stars started to appear on magazine covers, sunglasses took over.

Technology and fashion have made eyewear the most keenly styled accessory for the competitive rider. Since the 1980s, coloured plastic and mirrored lenses have furnished the faces of the peloton. Ranging from the screen, to the fly-eye, with candy colours and radical geometry, and every variation of reflection, refraction and spectral effects, they are essential to a convincing appearance on a bike.

Headwear

Early cyclists favoured the flying helmet, or a woollen cap, reaching for whatever would shade or wrap them.

Some time in the 1930s the cycling cap appeared. A small peaked cloth cap, almost disposable in its construction, became the defining headwear of the racing cyclist. Deceptively simple, the cap can provide shelter, shade or warmth, but most of all a prominent little arc of advertising right over the face of the winner. A woollen winter version has a deep cuff that can be pulled down over the neck, usually seen in Belgium. Worn tight down, or high like a chef's hat, peak forward

or back, even under a helmet, they were there on top of all the great riders throughout the twentieth century. Sadly, they have now been replaced by a branded baseball cap on the podium, the tragic abandonment of a distinctive cycling accessory.

The cycling helmet began to appear in the 1940s as the sausage, or hairnet, style, which was a set of joined leather tubes. It was famously worn by Jean 'Leatherhead' Robic. The hard hat appeared in the 1980s, a shell covering an impact-resistant crown. Helmets were made compulsory in 2003, following the death of Andrei Kivilev after a crash. Until then, most of the peloton rode bareheaded or with a cap, personal

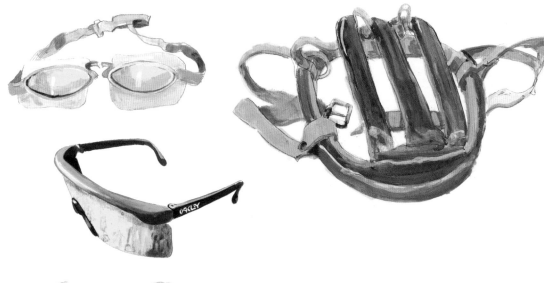

French goggles, elastic and rubber with tinted glass, 1930s

Oakley Blades, 1990s: the arrival of garishly coloured plastic

Himalaya Super Universal Lunettes, issued to the whole peloton in the 1960s

ABOVE
Primitive leather 'hairnet' helmet, made famous by Jean 'Leatherhead' Robic

OPPOSITE
Endangered by the spread of the baseball cap, the classic cycling headgear

attitude to risk and, later, aerodynamics deciding what was worn.

The form of the helmet is
constantly being refined in pursuit
of the ideal profile. Early Darth
Vader-inspired models and simple
basin shapes gave way to complex
mouldings with multiple perforations
and elaborate sculptural patterns.

The time-trial helmet demonstrated the most extreme commitment to a streamlined profile. The
extravagantly pointed shells of the
1990s had no protective function at
all – they were simply intended to
offer a better flow of air across the
rider. For record attempts, experiments were made with helmets that
engulfed the whole upper torso.

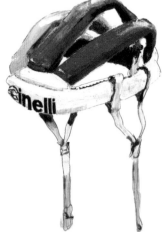

Shorts

Those who don't cycle are often alarmed by the sharpness of the saddle and slightly fascinated by the prominent pad in the shorts.

The first riders made do with woollen knickers, the plus fours of the sportsman. As the sport developed, padding was tailored into the seat, which helped, but the thick seams were an irritation. A chamois-leather pad was inserted, bringing relief to the contact points affected. Chamois care became part of the lore of cycling, as the soft glove leather needs to be treated carefully to retain its supple qualities.

Woollen knickers gave way to woollen shorts, but creasing and bunching exactly where you didn't want it made the pad even more necessary. The arrival of lycra in the 1980s tightened everything up, but the pad remained, becoming increasingly synthetic as technology provided something more efficient and less demanding than chamois.

Lycra shorts usually have braces, making them 'bibs', so that you don't get a bare back when leaning forward.

OPPOSITE
(CLOCKWISE FROM FAR LEFT)
Cinelli, 1980s, identical in form to the leather helmets of the 1930s, but made from coloured plastic.

Italian national team shell helmet, 1990.

Yellow helmet accessorizing the *maillot jaune*, 2016.

The lengths to which Lance Armstrong would go to win were demonstrated by this time-trial helmet from 1999. It had no protective purposes at all, being simply a foil to streamline his head.

Briko time-trial shell, 2000.

Bianchi Crono, 1997. Hand-formed titanium, used by the Russian Evgeni Berzin in time trials.

Shoes

The first models resembled old-fashioned leather footballs, laced and with leather soles. Light leather pumps, perforated for ventilation and stiffened for more efficient pedalling, followed.

To make a better connection between shoe and pedal, a steel plate was fitted to the sole, grooved to engage with a ridge on the pedal. This plate was called a 'nail'.

With the introduction of clipless pedals, a cleat was fixed to the sole of the shoe which spring-loaded into the body of the pedal. These did away with toe straps, but lost their tightening action. To tighten these shoes a ratchet mechanism was fitted to the shoe: sprinters tighten their feet hard down to the pedal as they prepare to launch themselves into the last few hundred metres.

The development of the shoe traces the inevitable progression from natural fibres to carbon, via plastic. Some modern shoes are little more than a carbon sock with a cleat on the bottom. Shoe covers, however, provide some protection from the elements. They also offer a more streamlined profile, and accessorize with the rest of a team's kit to complete the look.

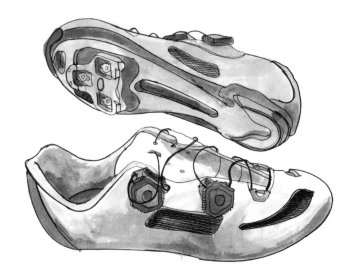

Shoes, leather and perforated, with maple wood soles, 1970s
Synthetic uppers with carbon soles, 2010

Race Radio

In the early years of strictly individual effort, riders were isolated for long periods of time, across huge stages. Communication was sporadic: passing cars might monitor their progress, and unannounced checkpoints would ensure their adherence to the route, but really they were on their own.

As stage races became team affairs, and tactics more collective, communications became crucial to the conduct of the race. Knowing where the breakaway is, and who is in it, controlling gaps, and knowing just where the contentious riders are has huge consequences on how you ride your race. A chalk board held up by the pillion passenger on a motorcycle, the *ardoisière*, was for years the only way to read the race. Essential information on the leader and the gaps would be held up in front of the peloton.

Mobile phones were seen in jersey pockets for a while, and in 2000 Lance Armstrong's team is reported to have phoned their doctor/'drug czar' Michele Ferrari mid-stage for his assessment of Marco Pantani's potential to do damage to Armstrong.

The development of lightweight mobile communications has brought race radio to sport. No longer does a rider have to drop back to the team car, hang on to the door and have a word with his *directeur sportif*. An earpiece delivers all the information that the team can glean: the gaps, who is where, and what should be done about it. Since its introduction in the 1990s race radio has been controversial. Does it make racing boring, when everyone knows who's in the breakaway, and whether they need to be brought back? A rider is constantly coached, his initiative is subordinated to the control of the team, and elements of the unknown are removed from the equation of the race. Or, are they a valuable aid to team tactics and do they keep riders safe when it is still possible to go over the edge unnoticed? The UCI is ambivalent, tentatively suggesting a ban, but repeatedly relenting under pressure from the teams. While this goes on though, the *ardoisière* is still out in front on the motorbike.

Race radio earpiece, the manager in your ear, a controversial accessory since 2000

Pharmacy

Professional cycle racing seems, unfortunately, to have become the poster-boy for doping in sport. The endurance needed for stage racing, and the demands of repeated recovery, might explain why it seems to occupy the front line of competitive drug taking.

The sport first came to the attention of the police in 1896, when Choppy Warburton, a British coach, was blamed for the death of one of his riders, Arthur Linton, after the Bordeaux–Paris race. Three of Choppy's boys were thought to have died from his assistance by the time he was relieved from his coaching position. (In a picturesque meeting of sport, technology and art, Henri de Toulouse-Lautrec featured Warburton in his poster for the Simpson Lever Chain, in the mid-1890s.)

With some of the early casualties of chemicals it was not clear whether they were doped or poisoned, the only difference between the two seeming to be the intention behind the dose and who administered it. It was the early days of pharmacy as well as cycling, and alarming combinations were recklessly swallowed: heroin, strychnine and chloroform were all taken as tonics, along with copious amounts of alcohol. The effects sought at this time seem to have been anaesthetic rather than performance-enhancing, with huge stage lengths, midnight starts and medieval road conditions making riding appallingly harsh.

In the beginning, there were no proscribed substances – the pharmacy cupboards were wide open, and full advantage was taken. In 1924 the Pélissier brothers, Henri and Francis, declared that they 'ran on dynamite', and Fausto Coppi was quite open about his reliance on 'la Bomba' (a mix of caffeine, cola and amphetamines): drugs were a casually confessed open secret. An ongoing series of collapses, retirements and occasional deaths, however, haunted the professional peloton, forcing regulation upon the sport, beginning in the mid-1960s, and slowly forensic policing of controlled substances became an increasingly intrusive part of racing. Producing urine on demand became another skill required of the professional rider. As chemistry and elite sport both evolved, the quality and sophistication of the drugs on offer increased, and the ad hoc consumption of homemade concoctions gave way to a ruthlessly scientific dark side of high-tech assistance.

A celebrated quartet from the 1990s with some stats.

Lance Armstrong's mea culpa, on *The Oprah Winfrey Show*, 2013.

67%

EPO

57.6% / hematocrit

Poisoned pigeon pie, bad fish – all sorts of excuses were offered for dodgy samples. The war on drugs was stepped up and the imperative to avoid detection increased as doping became unacceptable.

By 1998 less than 10 per cent of the peloton was thought to be free from doping, with EPO (erythropoietin) having emerged as the pharmaceutical of choice, boosting, as it did, the production of red blood cells.

The Festina Affair of 1998 meant it was no longer possible to ignore the elephant in the peloton, as the doping regimes of whole teams,

elaborate supply routes and bitter subterfuge of drug-assisted competition was subjected to very public scrutiny. The list of doped riders exposed by their A sample or B sample, confessing in their memoirs, or found with banned substances or drug paraphernalia became endless, and inevitable. High-profile exposés and mid-race expulsions became commonplace, culminating in the prime-time confession in 2013 of the world's most successful sportsman, Lance Armstrong, after years of belligerent denials in the face of dogged investigations and laboratory testing.

Undoubtedly, cycling has been damaged by its drug-fuelled past and persistent relapses. It is hard to take today's race seriously when the winner of last year's edition is still being decided in court. Roadside taunting, public suspicion of any outstanding performance and the undermining of past achievements all serve to leave a sport continually in doubt, as any result is always conditional on a blood test.

Musette

An enduring cycling classic, the *musette* is the disposable cotton bag held out at feed stations containing a packed lunch. Another perfect advertising format, it is a simple cotton rectangle with a narrow strap. Not even carbon can improve its function. It does, however, provide a frisson of risk in the way it is dangled to be snatched at by the rider, with potential for accidents if its swing is not controlled carefully. Lance Armstrong was dramatically floored by a rogue *musette* on Luz Ardiden in the Pyrenees in 2003.

Newspapers

As hot as it might get going up a mountain, the wind chill from descending from 3,000m (10,000ft) at 100km/h (62mph) is intense. For many years, at the top of the col newspapers were held out for riders, who stuffed them into the front of their shirts as improvised insulation.

Lexicon

A selection of terms that will help you talk like a pro even if you can't ride like one. If you are the last to see the *flamme rouge* you are the *lanterne rouge*. At the back of the race comes the 'broom wagon'. And if you meet the broom wagon, you've probably 'bonked'.

A

à bloc: To ride with total commitment. Risky, as it leaves nothing in reserve.

ardoisière: The person holding the chalkboard on the back of a motor-cycle in front of a race, giving the race leader and gaps. Named for the slate that the board was made from.

arrivée: The finish line.

autobus: A large group of riders with no hope of winning, grouped together for mutual support, the aim being to avoid elimination. Often seen in the mountains, usually made up of sprinters.

B

baroudeur-rouleur:
One of the legendary categories of rider defined on the topography of Europe. A *rouleur* can race over rolling roads for long periods of time, but a *baroudeur-rouleur* is one with some added fight in him and the potential breakaway at the end of the day (*baroudeur* is French for 'fighter'). The difference between a *baroudeur-rouleur* and a *puncheur*, though, is too hard to explain.

Belgian pot: A crude mixture of drugs, often amphetamine, cocaine and heroin.

bibs: Shorts or tights with braces, essential to avoid an undesirable gap.

bidon: Water bottle.

blow up: To bonk.

bollito: Bonked (Italian).

bomba: Literally, 'bomb', in Italian. An amphetamine preparation, widely used in the early years of chemicals, notably by Fausto Coppi.

bonk: To fail due to exhaustion. There seem to be more synonyms in the cycling lexicon for exhaustion than for any other condition or situation.

breakaway: An individual or small group escaping from the bunch.
Usually caught up by the collective advantage of the peloton.

broom wagon: Vehicle following the race to pick up abandons and riders subject to elimination. Often fitted with brooms to identify it. The iconic broom wagon is a Citroën H van, the corrugated classic.

C

cadence: Revolutions of the pedals.

caravan: Procession of commercial opportunities that precede the Tour de France. A collection of bizarre and extravagant floats hurling promotional trinkets into the crowds.

chain gang: Training group that takes itself very seriously.

chapeau!: Form of congratulation. An abbreviation of 'Coup de chapeau!' (hat's off!), an exclamation of respect for cycling achievement.

chute: Fall (French).

closing the door: Manoeuvring to obstruct a sprinter from passing you.

cooled: Bonked.

crack: To bonk.

crisi: Bonked (Italian).

criterium: Race of several laps around a closed circuit.

D

danseuse: French for 'dancer'. A rider who stands on the pedals and rides out of the saddle, usually when climbing.

domestique: Literally, a servant. A rider whose job it is to work in support of his team leader, drafting him, leading him through the field, and bringing him food and water.

dopage: Using pharmaceuticals to aid performance. A long history of doping exists in cycling, with its associated legislation, testing, bans, subterfuge, B testing, and visits to the 'station' at the end of the race to produce a sample.

drafting: Using the aerodynamic advantage of sheltering behind another rider.

drop: To accelerate away from another rider sufficiently for him not to be able to respond.

drillium: A now largely forgotten material that was widely used by compulsive weight-watchers, comprising any metal component or frame part into which holes are drilled to remove material, effectively lightening the bike. Most popular in chainrings, but also practised on seat posts, handlebars, brake levers and even through parts of the frame. The skill in making drillium is to know just how much mass you can remove before your component no longer has the strength to resist the forces at work upon it. A material usually improvised by amateur engineers, largely used in the 1960s and 1970s, it lives on with a few obsessive enthusiasts, but has really been made extinct by carbon and a more conscientious attitude to safety.

E

echelon: The most efficient and elegant arrangement of a peloton in windy conditions, a staggered line running diagonally down the road.

EPO: Erythropoietin. A blood booster; a synthetic hormone that stimulates the bone marrow to produce more red blood cells. More red blood cells means more oxygen which means increased endurance. Available since 1990, it replaced the previous tiresome ritual of actually removing blood, oxygenating it and

re-transfusing it back into the body, which was the previous practice of the cheating athlete.

F

false flat: A deceptive stretch on a climb, where it appears to level off, suggesting the summit, when in fact the gradient will ramp up again. *Falso piano* in Italian.

feed zone: Sanctioned area for refreshment on a stage race. Pick-up station for *musettes*.

Festina: Swiss watch manufacturer, sponsor of the Festina team through the 1990s. In cycling, though, the name is now synonymous with doping, after the Festina Affair of 1998, when one of the team's *soigneurs* was stopped driving what amounted to a mobile pharmacy into France three days before the beginning of the Tour de France.

flahute: Hardest of the hard. Inextricably linked with Belgium. There are those that admire the suffering in cycling more than anything, and they are in thrall to the notion of the *flahute*. He epitomizes the masochistic fantasies of the macho-cyclist. However much suffering you can imagine on two wheels, the *flahute* will take it, and just a bit more.

flamme rouge: Big red inflatable that marks one kilometre to go.

fondista: Allrounder (Italian).

French flat: A long stretch of road, seemingly level, but really a consistent imperceptible uphill gradient. Demoralizing to ride on.

fried: Bonked.

G

GC: General Classification. The overall leader of a stage race, that is,

the one with the lowest cumulative time. CG in French.

La Grande Boucle: 'The Big Loop': French name for the Tour de France.

gregario: Italian domestique.

grimpeur: Climber.

grupetto: see *autobus*

H

hematocrit: The measure of the percentage of red cells in the blood. Anything over 50 per cent is accepted as being evidence of blood doping.

hit the wall: To bonk.

hors catégorie: Or HC. Literally, 'beyond category', a climb off the usual scale of severity. Rated by gradient, length and where it falls in the day's racing.

hors délai: Or HD. Elimination by falling outside the time limit for a stage.

hunger knock: Bonk.

K

knickers: Shorts that reach below the knees. Not underwear.

knock: Bonk.

L

lanterne rouge: Last rider on the road.

laughing group: see *autobus*

leadout: A rider bringing his sprinter to the front of the field, positioning him to make his attack.

leech: Persistent drafter,

reluctant to take a turn in the wind. Not good form.

M

magic spanner: A subtle form of cheating, where a rider holds onto a team car while a mechanic goes through the motions of working on his bike. The rider gets a rest, and a firm push off when he can no longer reasonably be seen to be towed by the car.

mankini: Unfortunately, this seems to have become the costume of choice for a lot of cycling fans. Seems to have replaced the strategically placed girl in a bikini, the traditional photo opportunity of the last century.

mechanical/motorized doping: A concealed motor. Obviously not race-legal. No one has yet been caught doing this, but suspicions have been widely aired, and performances scrutinized.

mur: Literally, wall. An intimidating climb.

musette: Feed bag.

N

neutral zone: An enforced non-competitive section of a race where pace is controlled behind a car.

O

off the back: Dropped, probably because you bonked.

off the front: Breaking away ahead of the group.

P

pace line: An organized arrangement of riders, taking turns at the front and then dropping back to join on the rear, rotating the lead. A collaboration that will ensure the best progress for the group, exploiting aerodynamics and reserving energy.

palmarès: A rider's success or record of achievement.

passista: An Italian *rouleur*.

pedalling circles/pedalling squares: Pedalling efficiently and smoothly/fatigued, erratic pedalling.

peloton: The mass of riders, either the largest group on the road, or the collective of racing cyclists.

prologue: A short time trial at the beginning of a stage race. Allows someone to wear a leader's jersey on Stage 1.

puncheur: A rider specializing in rolling terrain with short, steep climbs. The Spring classics and many one-day races suit this type of rider, but the long climbs of a stage race will probably defeat him.

Q

queen stage: The hardest stage of a stage race.

R

road rash: Physical evidence of a *chute*.

rotating weight: A physical law that, briefly, means that light wheels are best. Weight that is turning while the bike moves forward – this means the wheels and the pedals, effectively – resists acceleration, and the heavier it is the more it resists. The effect is more pronounced the faster you go, so it makes a bigger difference on the flat than when climbing.

rouleur: A rider who is strong over long undulating courses. Like a *puncheur*, but without the steepest bits.

S

sag wagon: The vehicle following the race to pick you up if your bonk is terminal.

scalatore: Climber (Italian).

scattista: An Italian *puncheur*.

soigneur: Carer. Feeding, clothing, cleaning and ensuring the wellbeing of the rider. Sometimes implicated in doping management as well.

sticky bottle: Similar to the magic spanner. If you are passed a bottle from a moving car, but hang on for just that bit longer than you need to, you can stop pedalling. Again, you have to judge just how long you can do it before it becomes too obvious.

succhia rotta: Wheel sucker. (Italian).

T

tifoso (pl. tifosi): Cycle-racing fans, usually reserved for Italians.

U

UCI: Union Cycliste Internationale, established 1900. The organizing body of international cycle racing. Writes the rules and enforces compliance.

V

velocista: Sprinter (Italian).

ventaglio: An Italian echelon.

volata: Sprint (Italian).

W

water carriers: Anglophone domestiques. Named for the duty, which is to fill their shirts with water bottles to distribute to the rest of their team.

wheelsucker: See **leech**

To Lubna and Roshan, with love, and with thanks
for allowing me the time to be out on a bike.

To the many friends, family and colleagues
who have helped me in my work.

My mother, Jon and Patrick.

Paul Neale and Angela Moore, Angus Hyland,
Lucy Rogers, Ian Bilbey, Andrew Grassie and Kitty
Beamish, Philip Hunt, Michelle Edwards, Jack Davidson,
Tim Millin, John Greenwood and Helen Megarry, Luke
Hayman, Véronique Rolland, Matteo Cassina, Lisa Slater
(logistical support on Crag Vale), the Chowdhary family,
Naweed and Afsan, Mr and Mrs Chowdhary.

Kai Zimmermann and Rymn Massand, for many things,
but notably logistical support on the Tourmalet,
Mont Ventoux and the Hautacam.

Rosa Nguyen and David Blamey, for many things,
including logistical support on the Peyresourde,
Superbagneres and the Col de Menté.

Philip Contos and Alex Coco for
making this eventually get done.

Dulwich Paragon Cycling Club, for miles of
inspirational and companionable riding.

*This book is dedicated
to my sister Jenny. If you
love doing something,
do it while you can.*

Francesco Moser's commitment
to streamlining led him to test
a helmet that included a fairing
covering his whole upper body,
1984.